To Emily Dickinson

I too am stuck Indoors
Emily – with only
my Fly-like Buzz –

but I stumble – on this
Alpine album Emily –
and it reminds me

of your Emotional Scale–
A Party at a Silent Table
For Scalpel – Needle –

Shadow Daisies – Sepia
Glacier – Bonnet flung down.
A Bird lights on this Loaf

Picks at Words to Swell
Poems. Your Candle –
accompanies the Sun –

by SOPHIE HERXHEIMER   1

Presentiment – is that long Shadow – on the Lawn –
Indicative that Suns go down –

The Notice to the startled Grass
That Darkness – is about to pass –

My Life had stood - a Loaded Gun -
In Corners - till a Day
The Owner passed - identified -
And carried Me away -

And now We roam in Sovreign Woods -
And now We hunt the Doe -
And every time I speak for Him
The Mountains straight reply -

And do I smile, such cordial light
Opon the Valley glow -
It is as a Vesuvian face
Had let it's pleasure through -

And when at Night - Our good Day done -
I guard My Master's Head -
'Tis better than the Eider Duck's
Deep Pillow - to have shared -

To foe of His - I'm deadly foe -
None stir the second time -
On whom I lay a Yellow Eye -
Or an emphatic Thumb -

Though I than He - may longer live
He longer must - than I -
For I have but the power to kill,
Without - the power to die -

I'll tell you how the Sun rose –
A Ribbon at a time –
The Steeples swam in Amethyst –
The news, like Squirrels, ran –
The Hills untied their Bonnets –
The Bobolinks – begun –
Then I said softly to myself –
'That must have been the Sun'!
But how he set – I know not –
There seemed a purple stile
That little Yellow boys and girls
Were climbing all the while –
Till when they reached the other side,
A Dominie in Gray –
Put gently up the evening Bars –
And led the flock away –

It is an honorable Thought
And makes One lift One's Hat
As One met sudden Gentlefolk
Upon a daily Street

That we've immortal Place
Though Pyramids decay
And Kingdoms, like the Orchard
Flit Russetly away

Tell all the truth but tell it slant —
Success in Circuit lies
Too bright for our infirm Delight
The Truth's superb surprise
As Lightning to the Children eased
With explanation kind
The Truth must dazzle gradually
    Or every man be blind —

The Mushroom is the Elf of Plants –
At Evening, it is not –
At morning, in a Truffled Hut
It stop upon a Spot

As if it tarried always
And yet its whole Career
Is shorter than a Snake's Delay
And fleeter than a Tare –

'Tis Vegetation's Juggler –
The Germ of Alibi –
Doth like a Bubble antedate
And like a Bubble, hie –

I feel as if the Grass was pleased
To have it intermit –
This surreptitious scion
Of Summer's circumspect.

They shut me up in Prose –
As when a little Girl
They put me in the Closet –
Because they liked me "still" –

Still! Could themself have peeped –
And seen my Brain – go round –
They might as wise have lodged a Bird
For Treason – in the Pound –

Himself has but to will
And easy as a Star
Look down opon Captivity –
And laugh – No more have I –

After great pain, a formal feeling comes –
The Nerves sit ceremonious, like Tombs –
The stiff Heart questions 'was it He, that bore,'
And 'Yesterday, or Centuries before'?

The Feet, mechanical, go round –
A Wooden way
Of Ground, or Air, or Ought –
Regardless grown,
A Quartz contentment, like a stone –

This is the Hour of Lead –
Remembered, if outlived,
As Freezing persons, recollect the Snow –
First – Chill – then Stupor – then the letting go –

I dwell in Possibility –
A fairer House than Prose –
More numerous of Windows –
Superior – for Doors –

Of Chambers as the Cedars –
Impregnable of eye –
And for an everlasting Roof
The Gambrels of the Sky –

Of Visitors – the fairest –
For Occupation – This –
The spreading wide my narrow Hands
To gather Paradise –

I started Early – Took my Dog –
And visited the Sea –
The Mermaids in the Basement
Came out to look at me –

And Frigates – in the Upper Floor
Extended Hempen Hands –
Presuming Me to be a Mouse –
Aground – opon the Sands –

But no Man moved Me – till the Tide
Went past my simple Shoe –
And past my Apron – and my Belt
And past my Boddice – too –

And made as He would eat me up –
As wholly as a Dew
Opon a Dandelion's Sleeve –
And then – I started – too –

And He – He followed – close behind –
I felt His Silver Heel
Opon my Ancle – Then My Shoes
Would overflow with Pearl –

Until We met the Solid Town –
No One He seemed to know –
And bowing – with a Mighty look –
At me – The Sea withdrew –

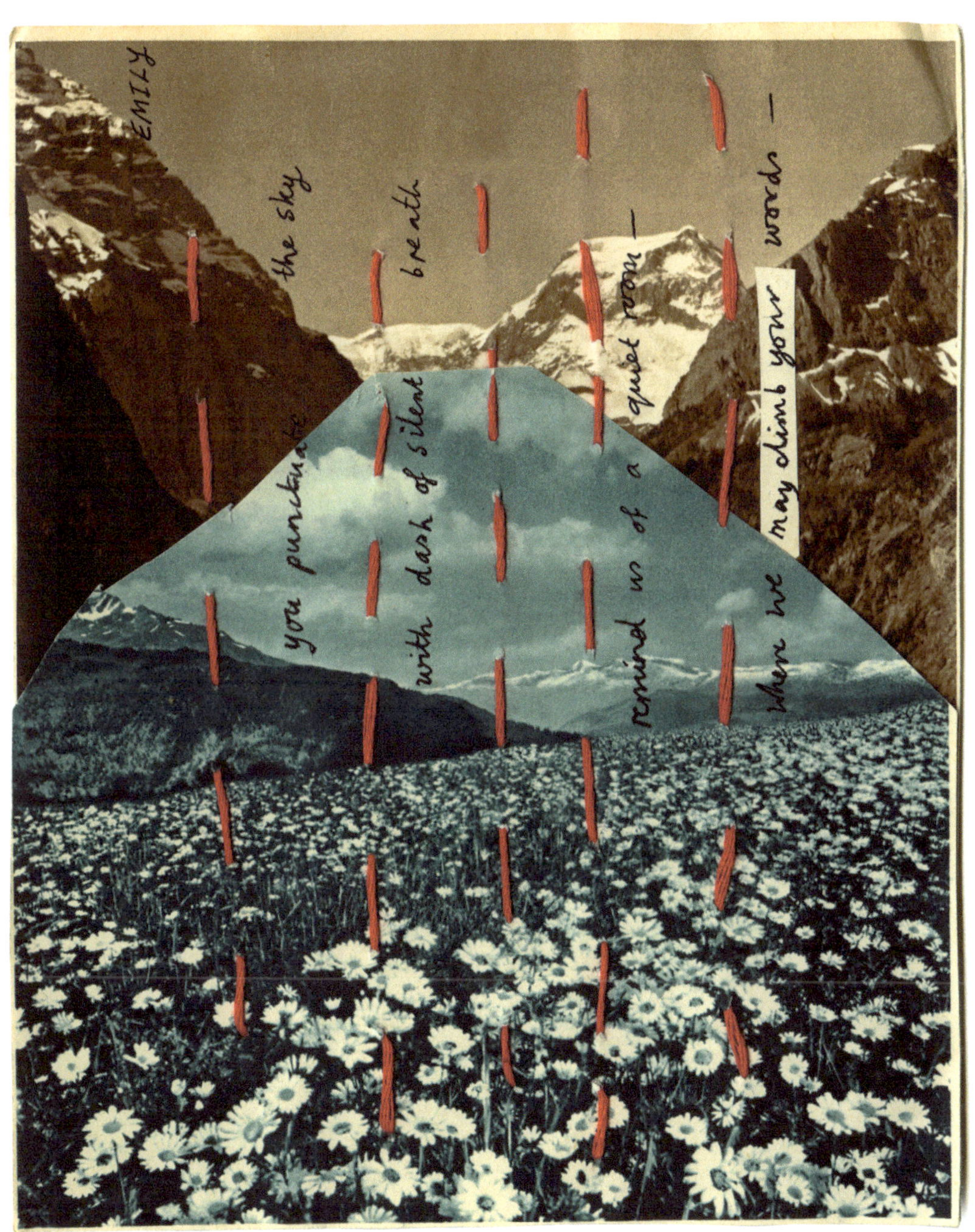

EMILY
the sky
you puncture
breath
with dash of silent
remind us of a
quiet room —
when we may climb your
words —

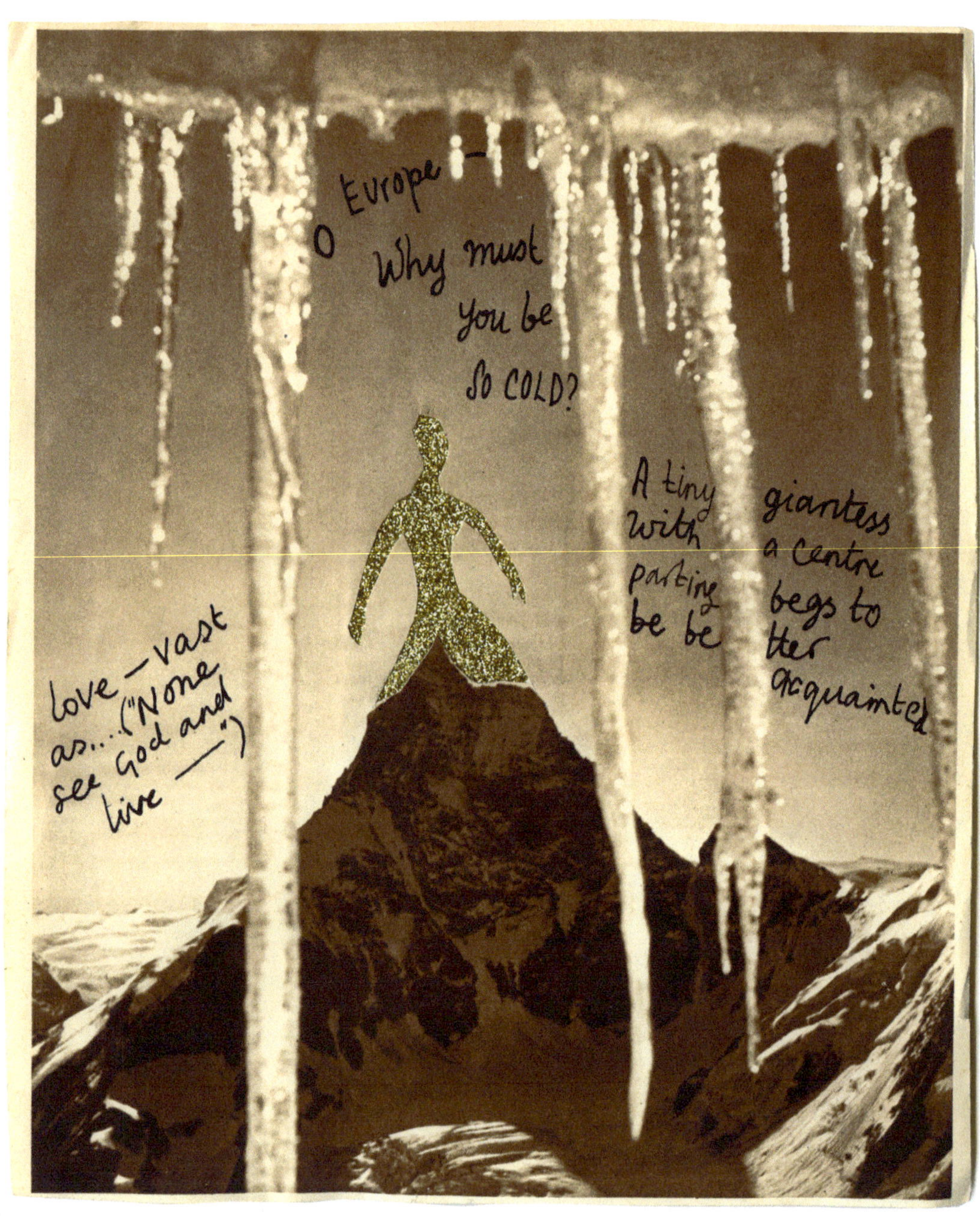

O Europe —
Why must
you be
so COLD?

A tiny   giantess
with   a centre
parting begs to
be be   tter
         acquainted

love — vast
as...("None
see God and
live — ")

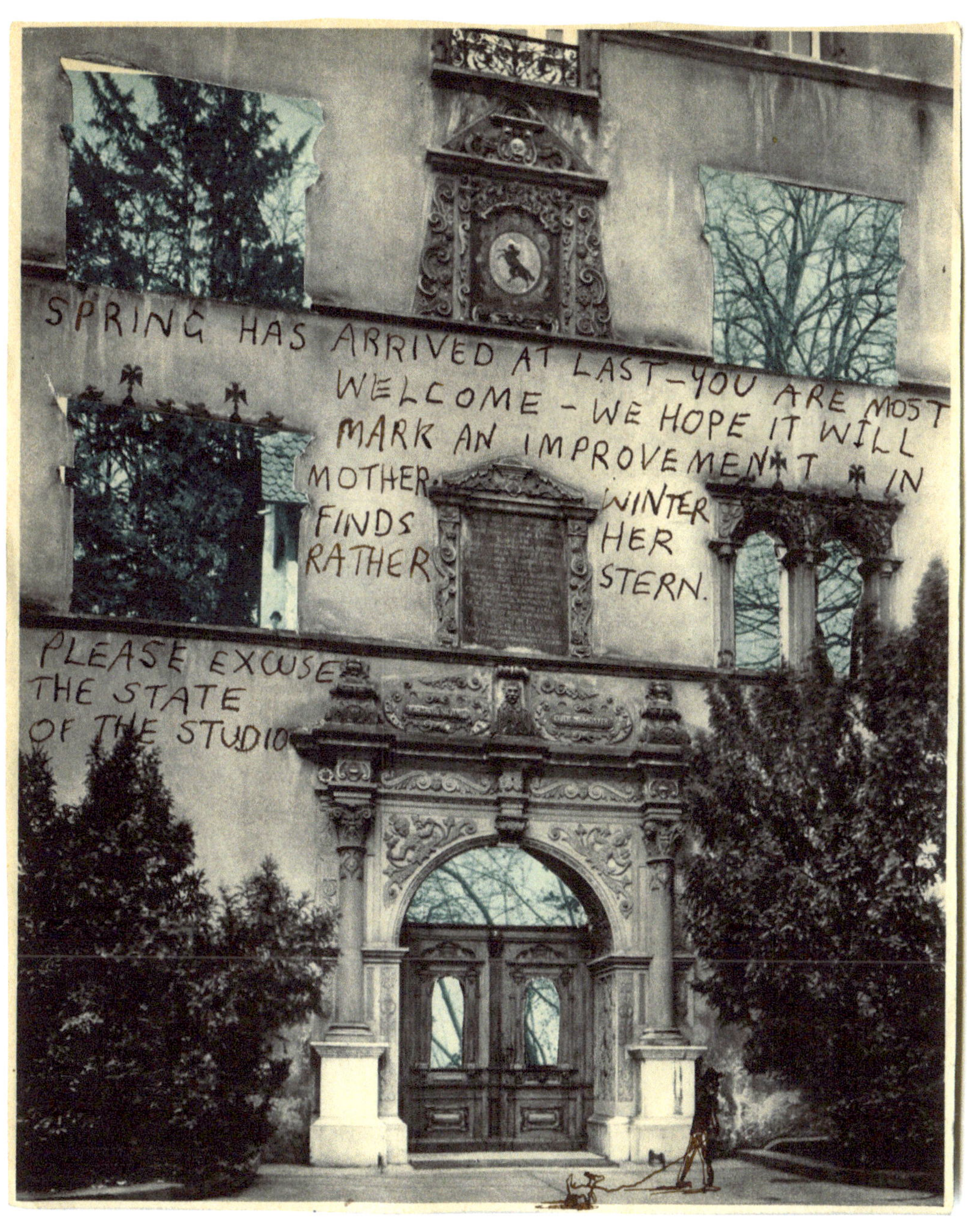

SPRING HAS ARRIVED AT LAST—YOU ARE MOST
WELCOME — WE HOPE IT WILL
MARK AN IMPROVEMENT IN
MOTHER
FINDS
RATHER
WINTER
HER
STERN.
PLEASE EXCUSE
THE STATE
OF THE STUDIO

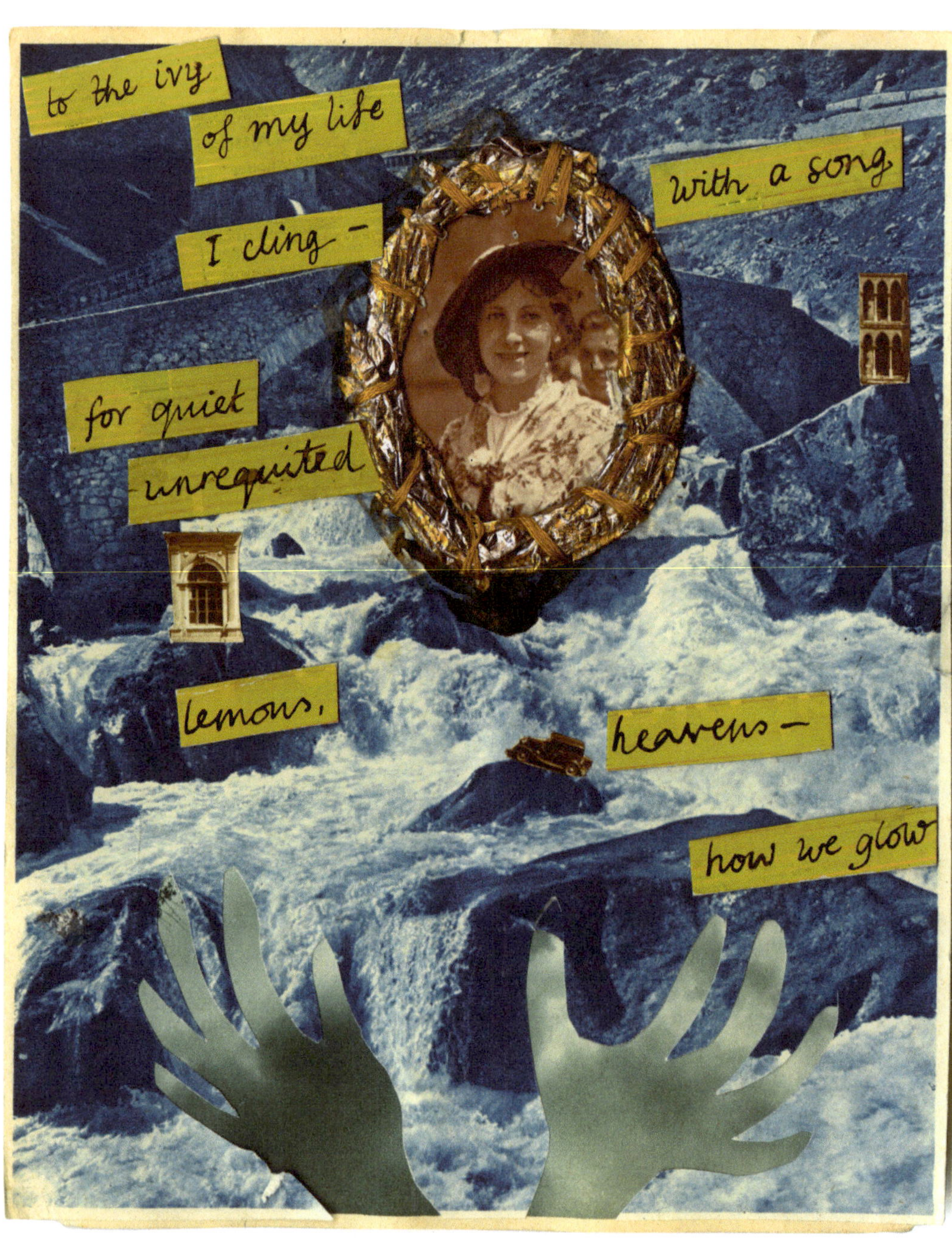

to the ivy
of my life
I cling —
with a song
for quiet
unrequited
lemons,
heavens —
how we glow

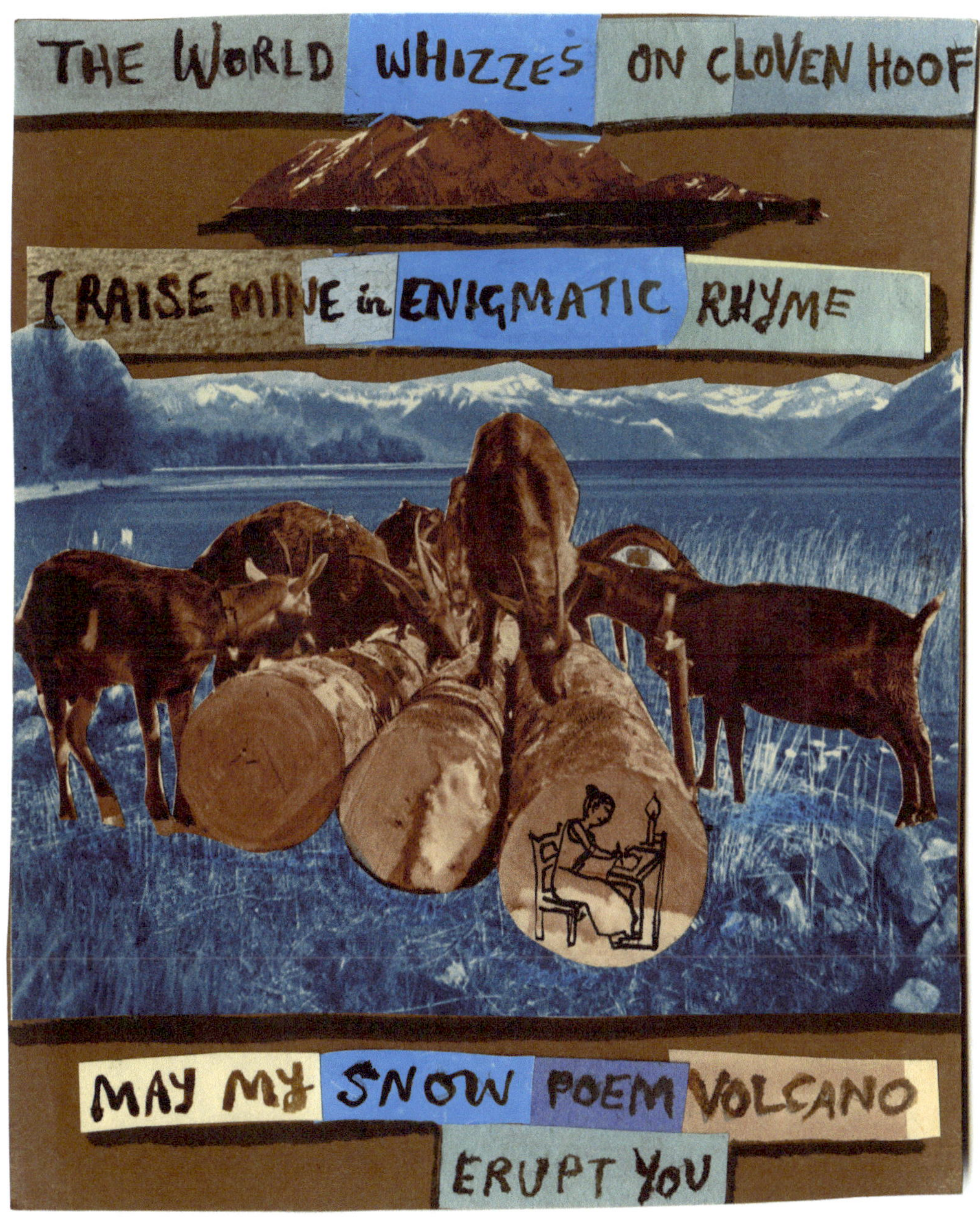

THE WORLD WHIZZES ON CLOVEN HOOF
I RAISE MINE in ENIGMATIC RHYME
MAY MY SNOW POEM VOLCANO
ERUPT YOU

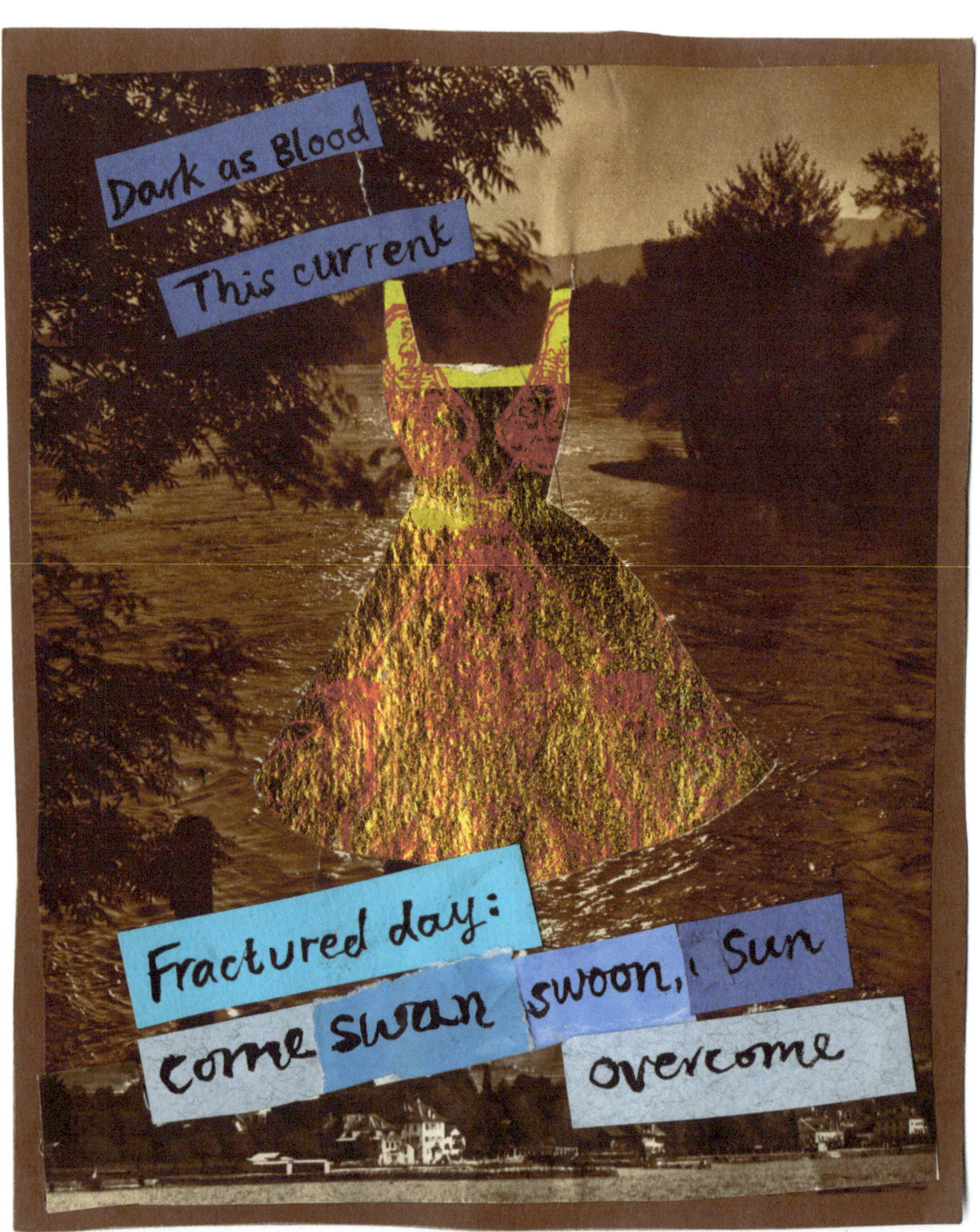
Dark as Blood
This current
Fractured day:
come swan swoon, Sun
overcome

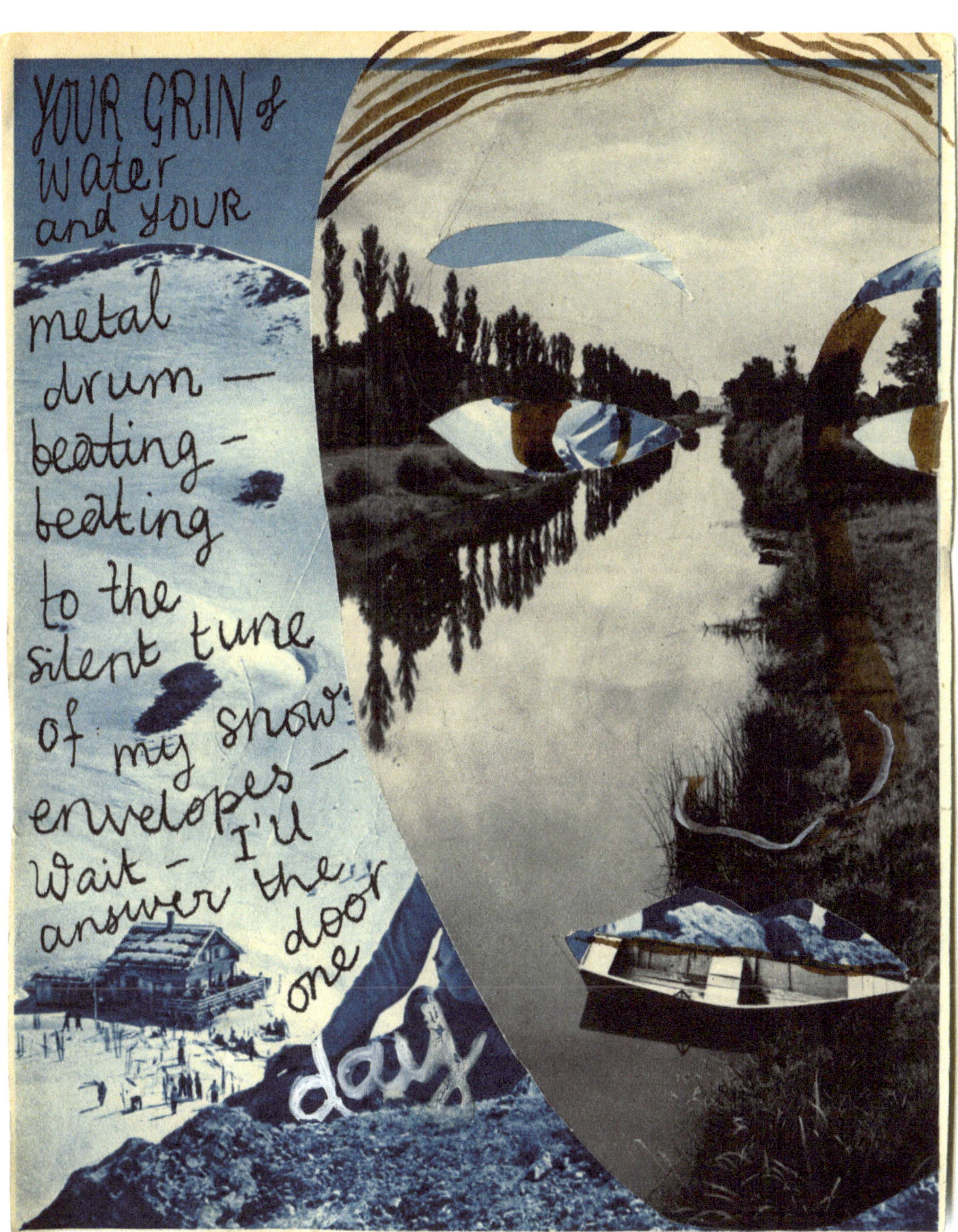
YOUR GRIN of
water
and YOUR

metal
drum —
beating —
beating
to the
silent tune
of my snow-
envelopes —
wait — I'll
answer the
door
one
day

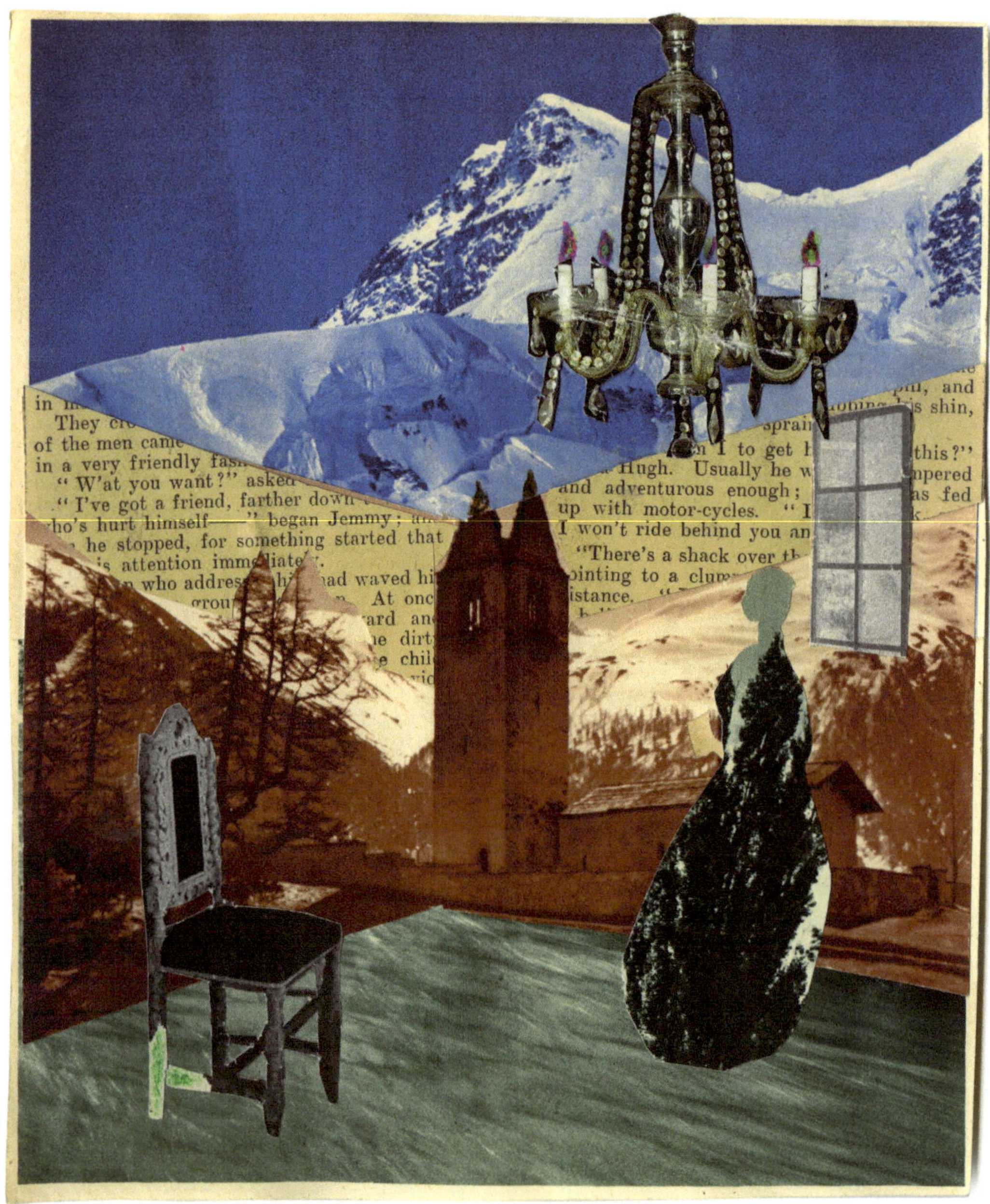

in
They cro
of the men came
in a very friendly fash
"W'at you want?" asked
"I've got a friend, farther down
who's hurt himself——" began Jemmy;
he stopped, for something started that
is attention immediat
who address h ad waved hi
grou
the dirt
e chil
him, and
his shin,
spra
n I to get h this?"
Hugh. Usually he w mpered
and adventurous enough; as fed
up with motor-cycles. "
I won't ride behind you an
"There's a shack over th
pointing to a clum
istance. "
ard an

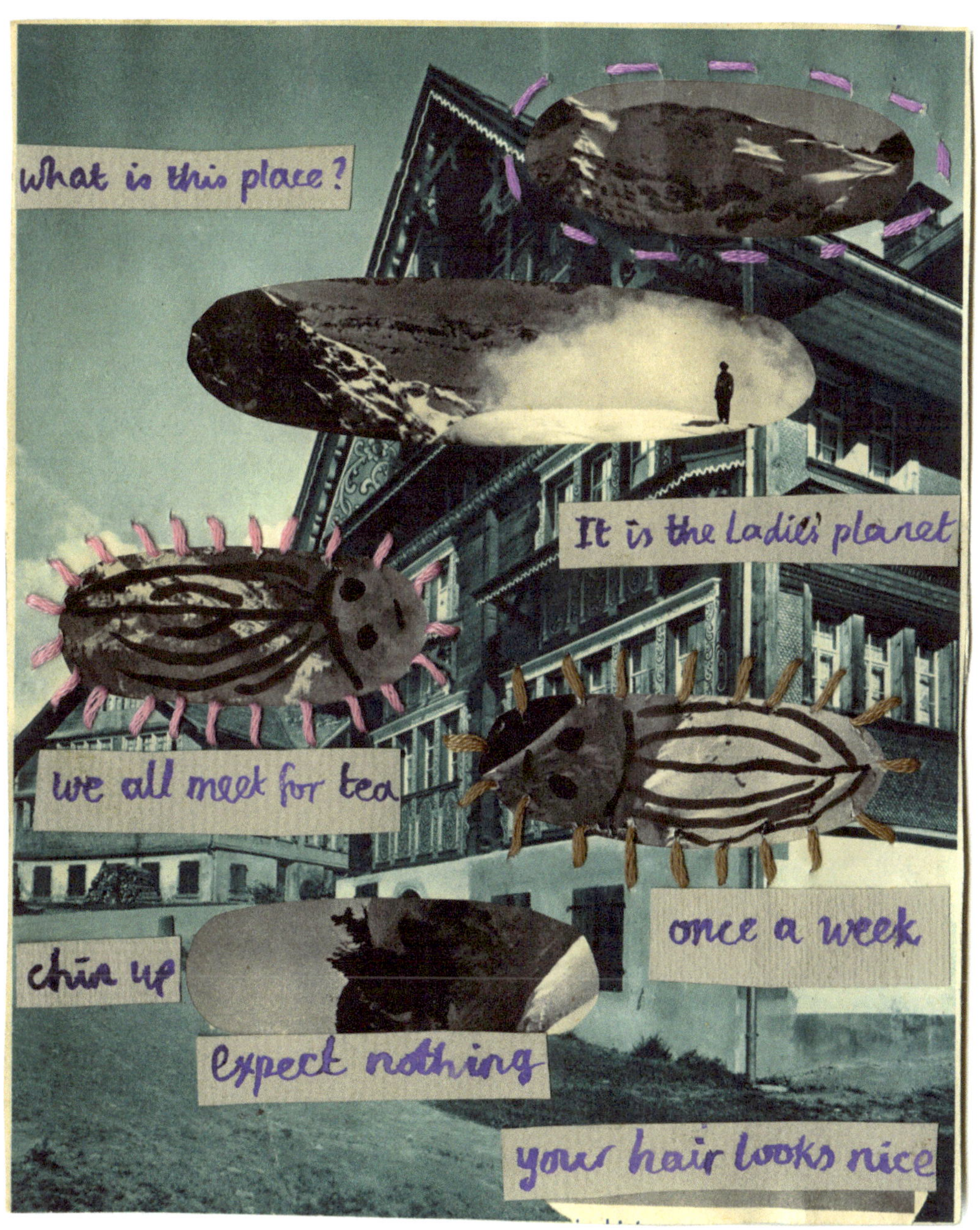

what is this place?
It is the ladies' planet
we all meet for tea
once a week
chin up
expect nothing
your hair looks nice

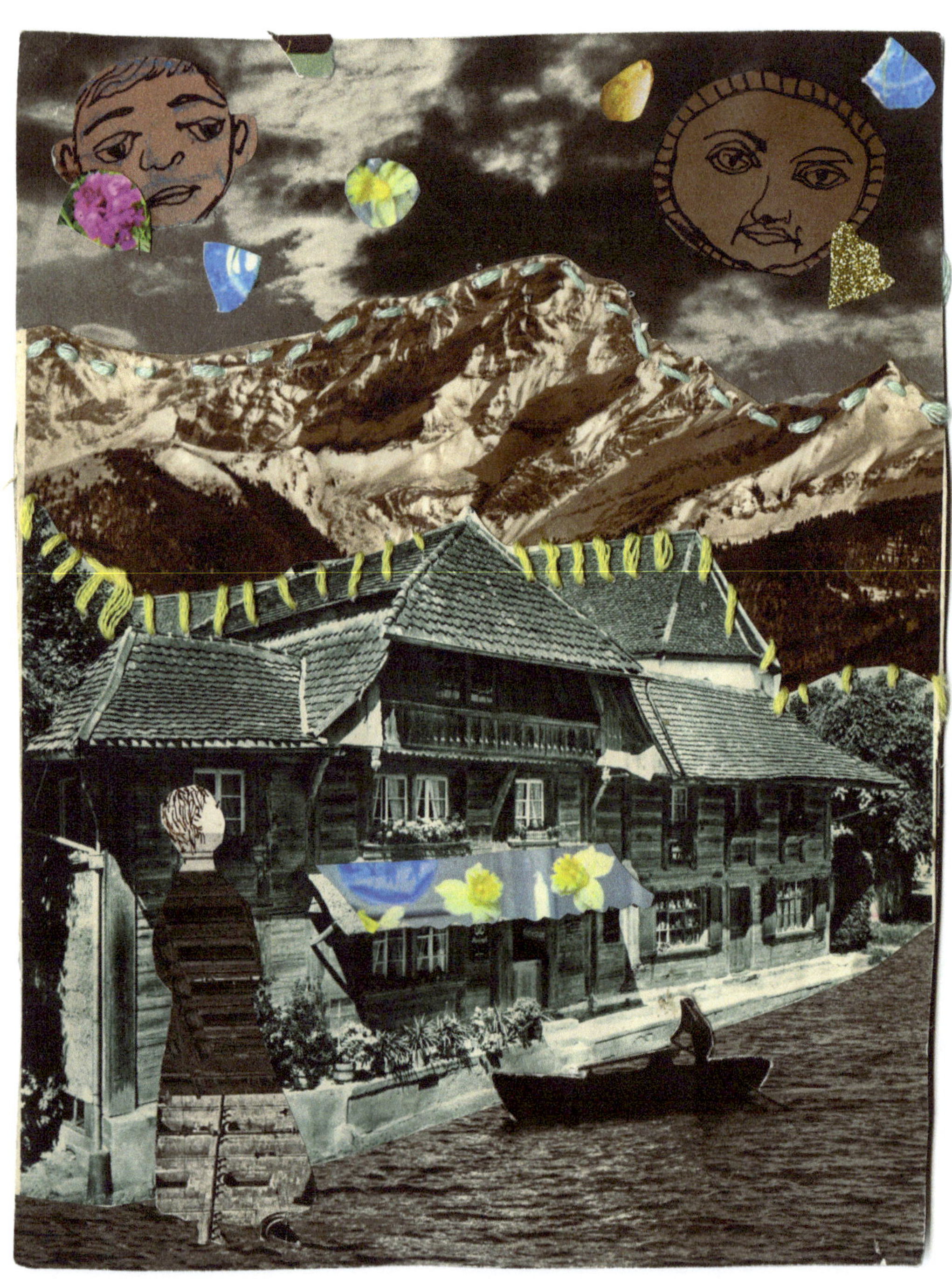

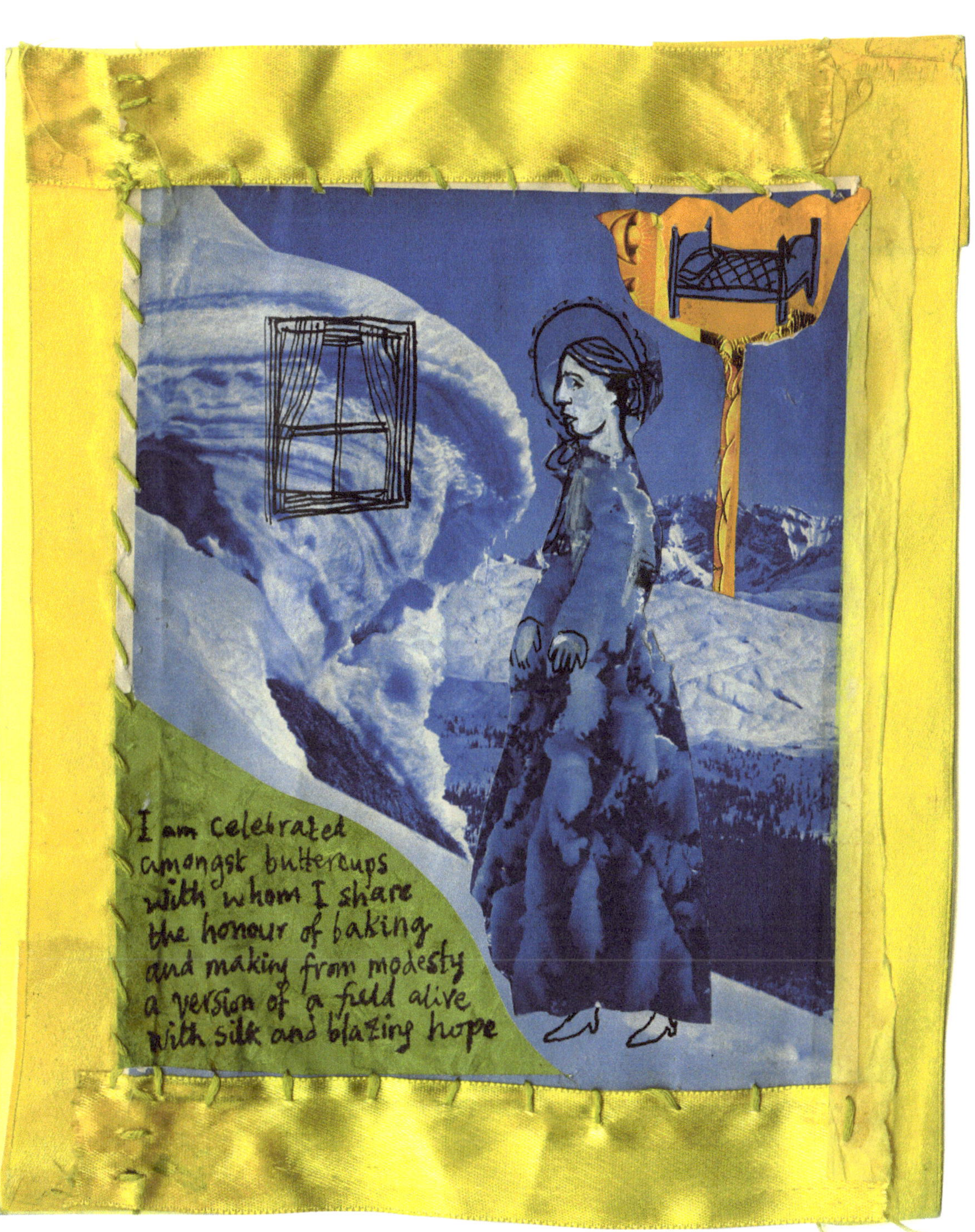
I am celebrated
amongst buttercups
with whom I share
the honour of baking
and making from modesty
a version of a field alive
with silk and blazing hope

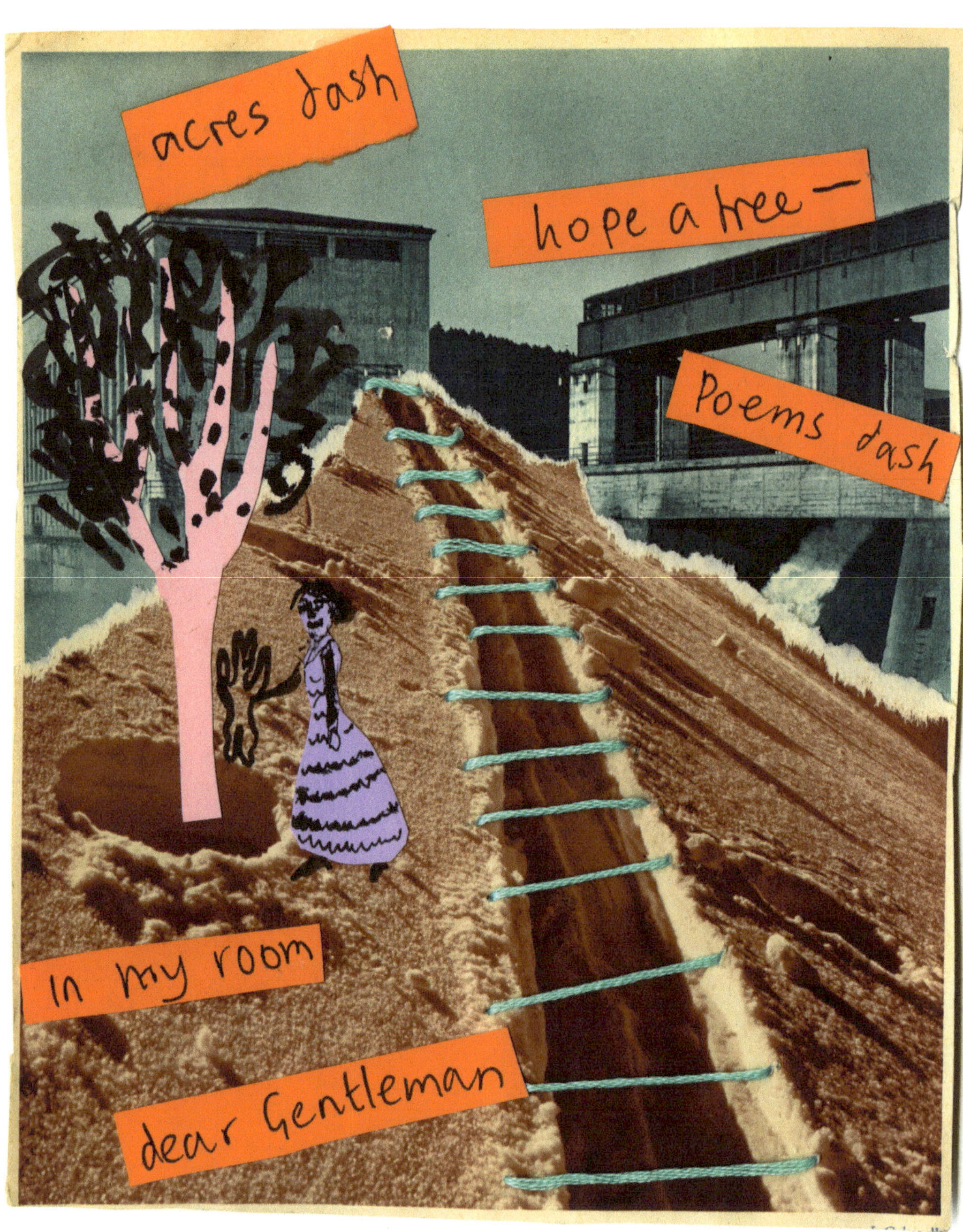

acres dash
hope a tree —
Poems dash
in my room
dear Gentleman

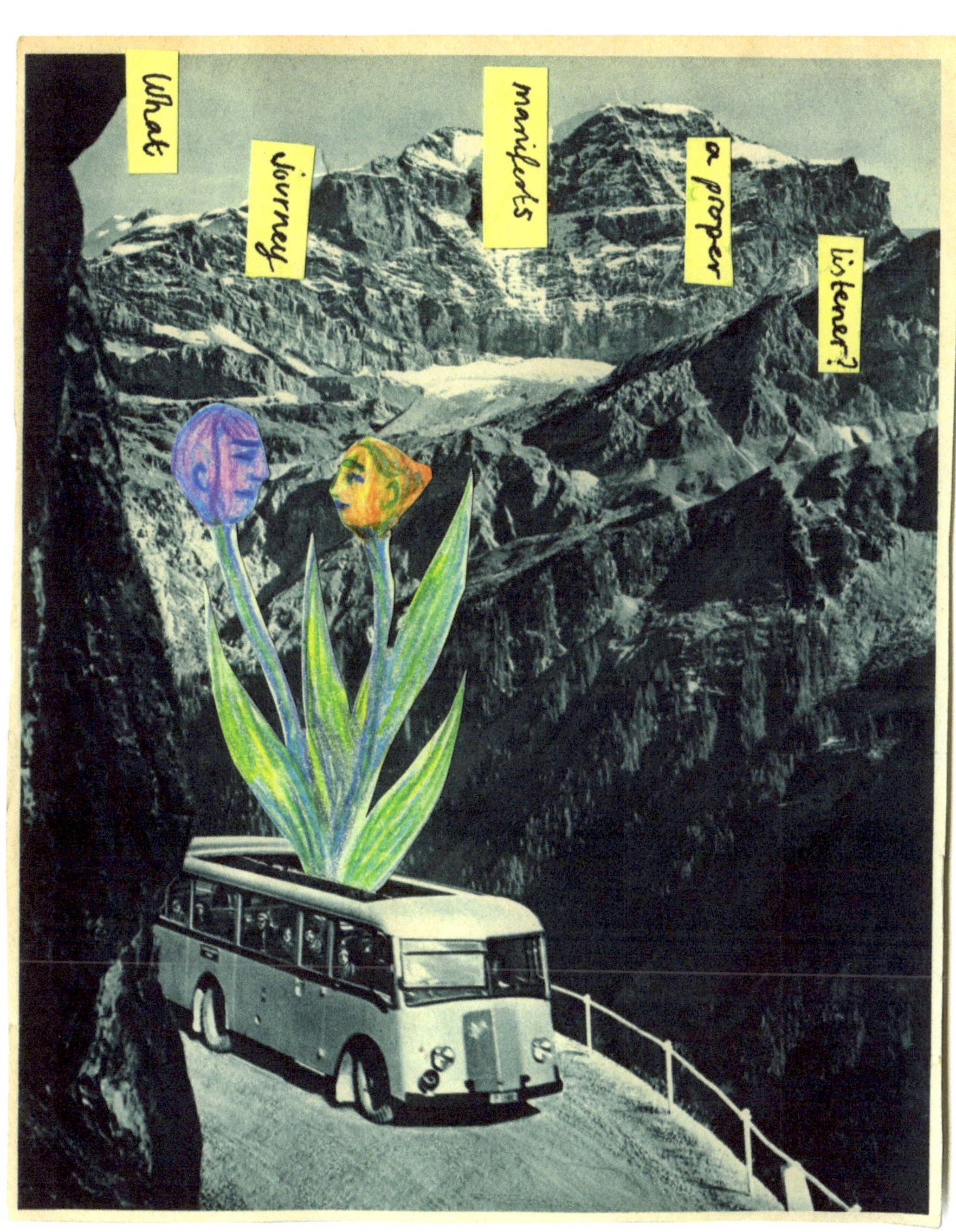

What
journey
manifests
a proper
listener?

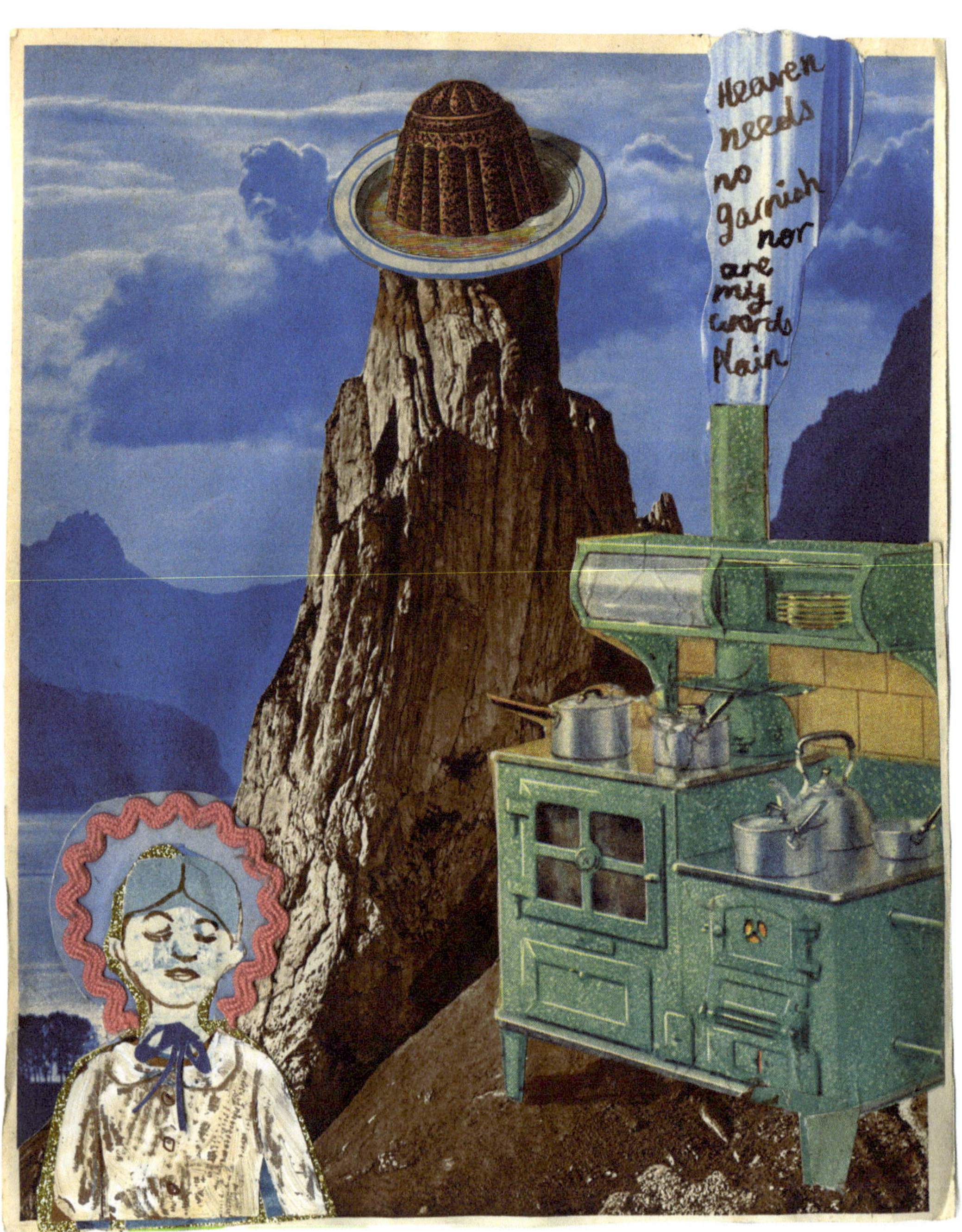

Heaven
needs
no
garnish
nor
are
my
words
plain

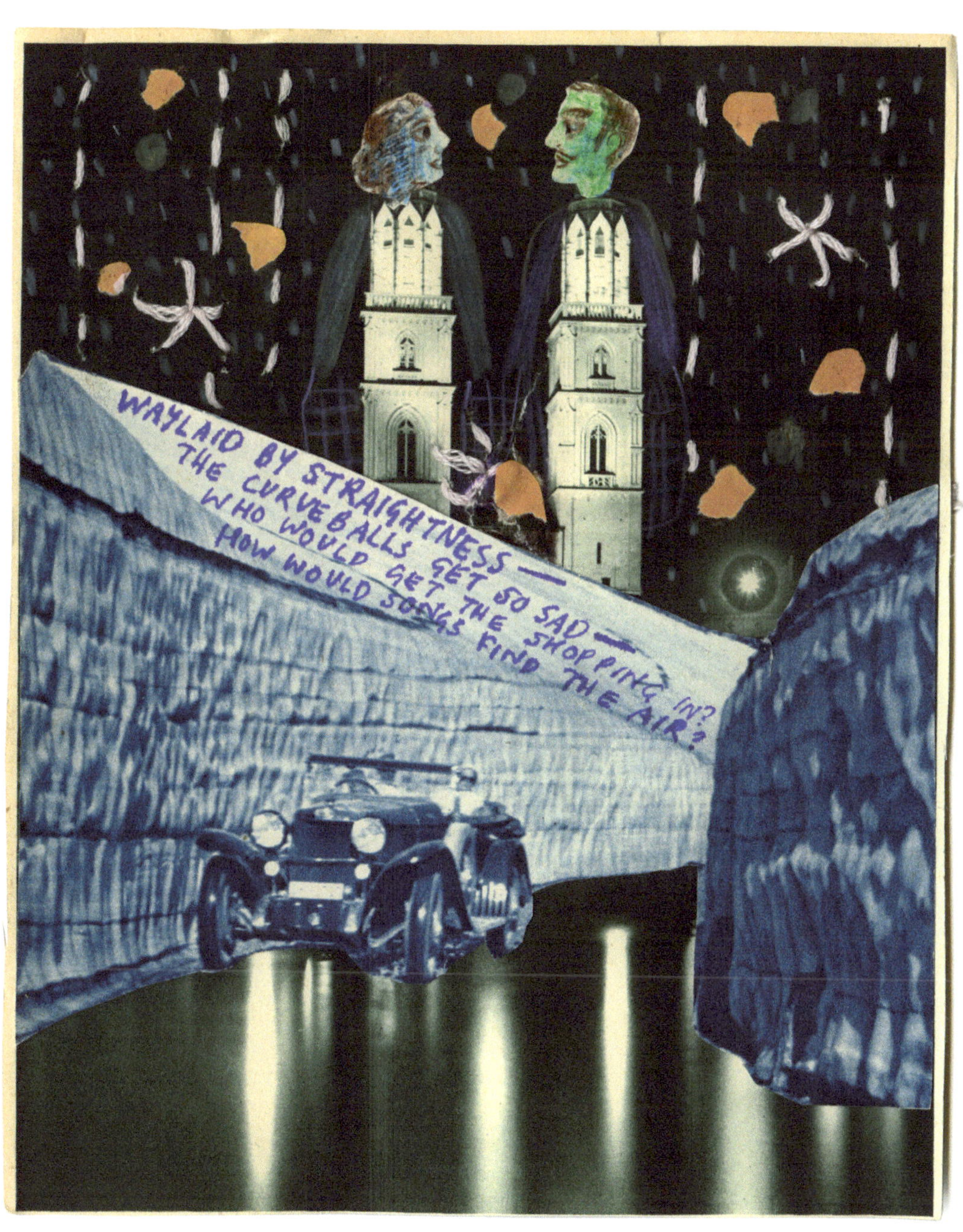

WAYLAID BY STRAIGHTNESS —
THE CURVEBALLS GET SO SAD —
WHO WOULD GET THE SHOPPING IN?
HOW WOULD SONGS FIND THE AIR?

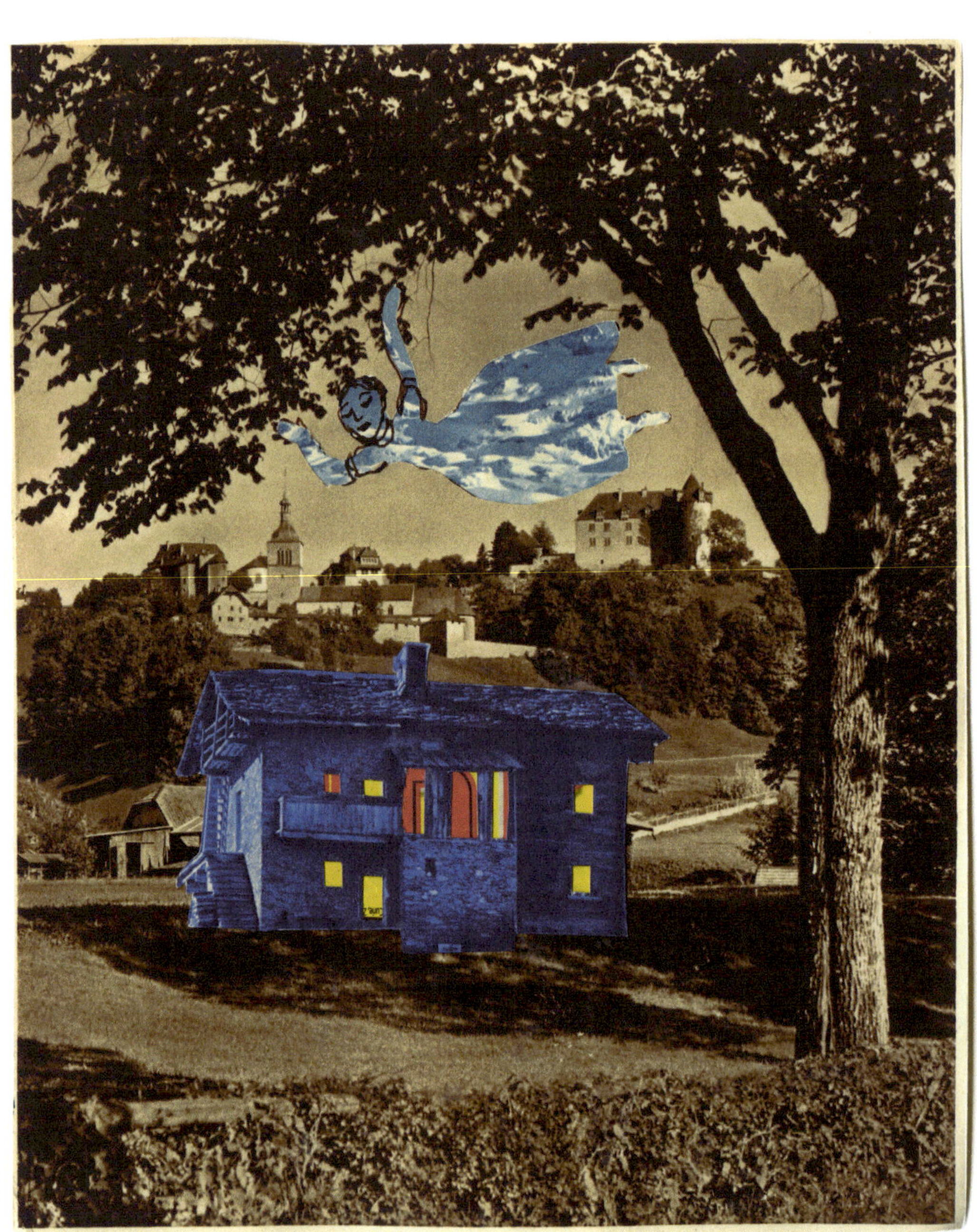

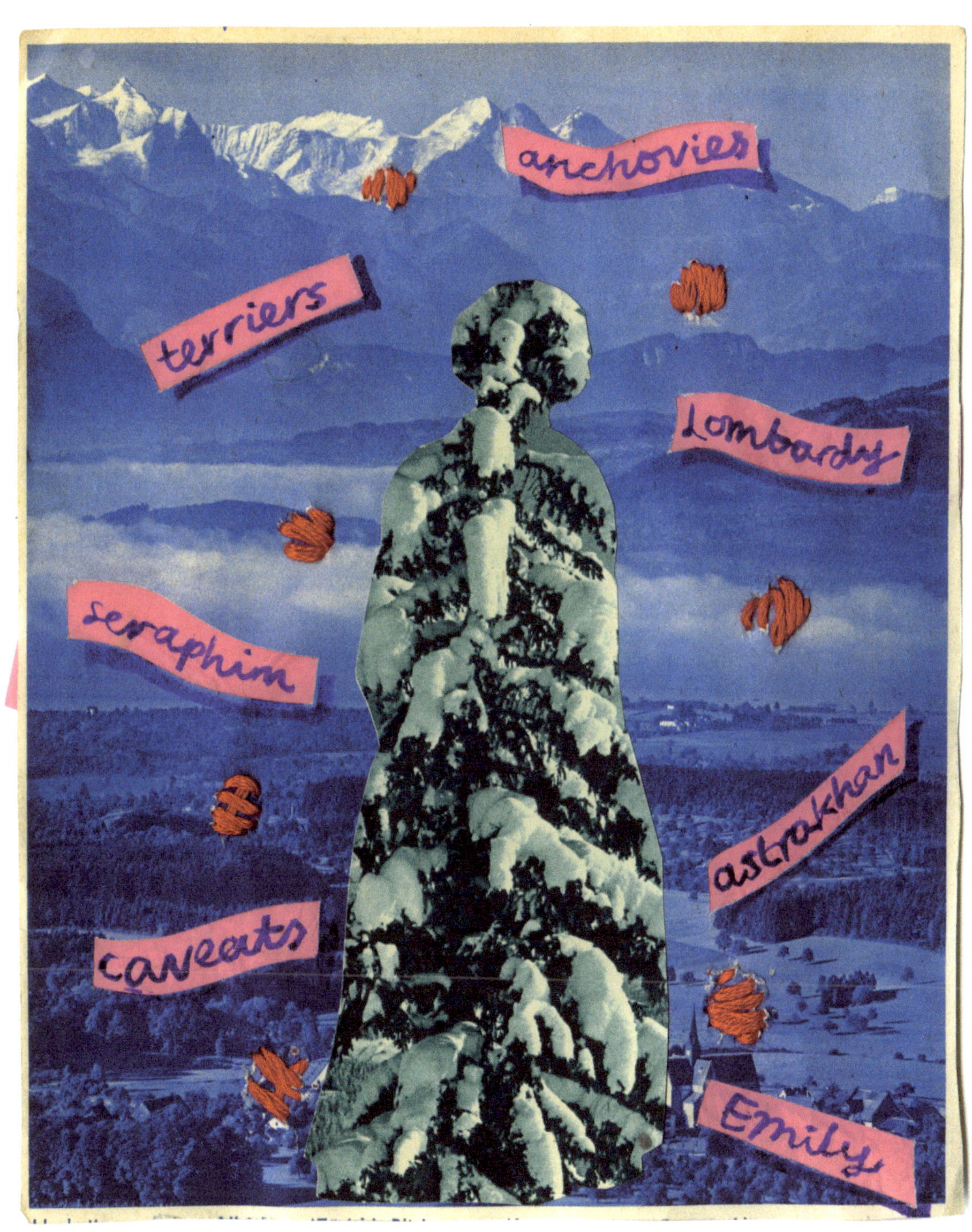

anchovies
terriers
Lombardy
seraphim
astrakhan
caveats
Emily

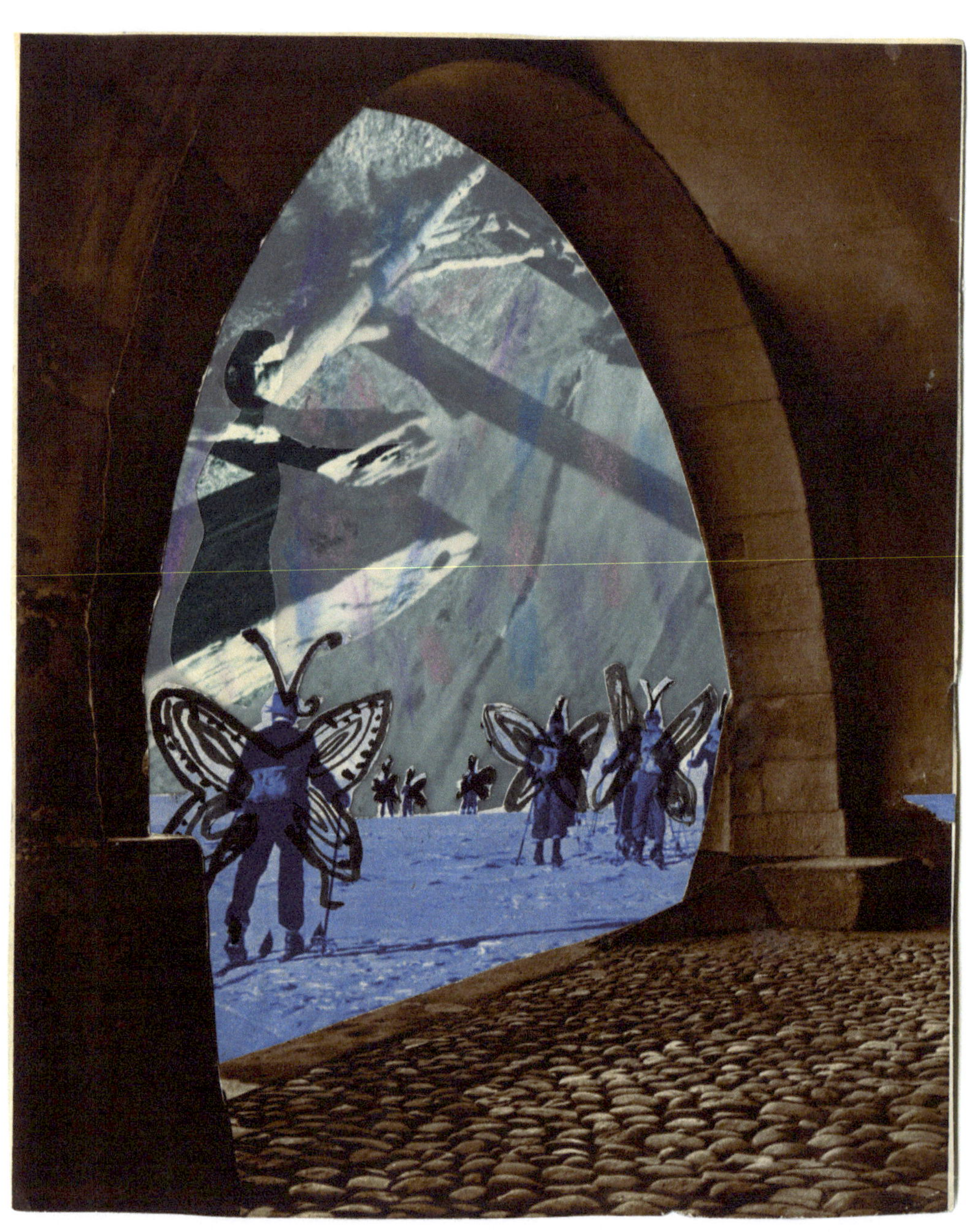

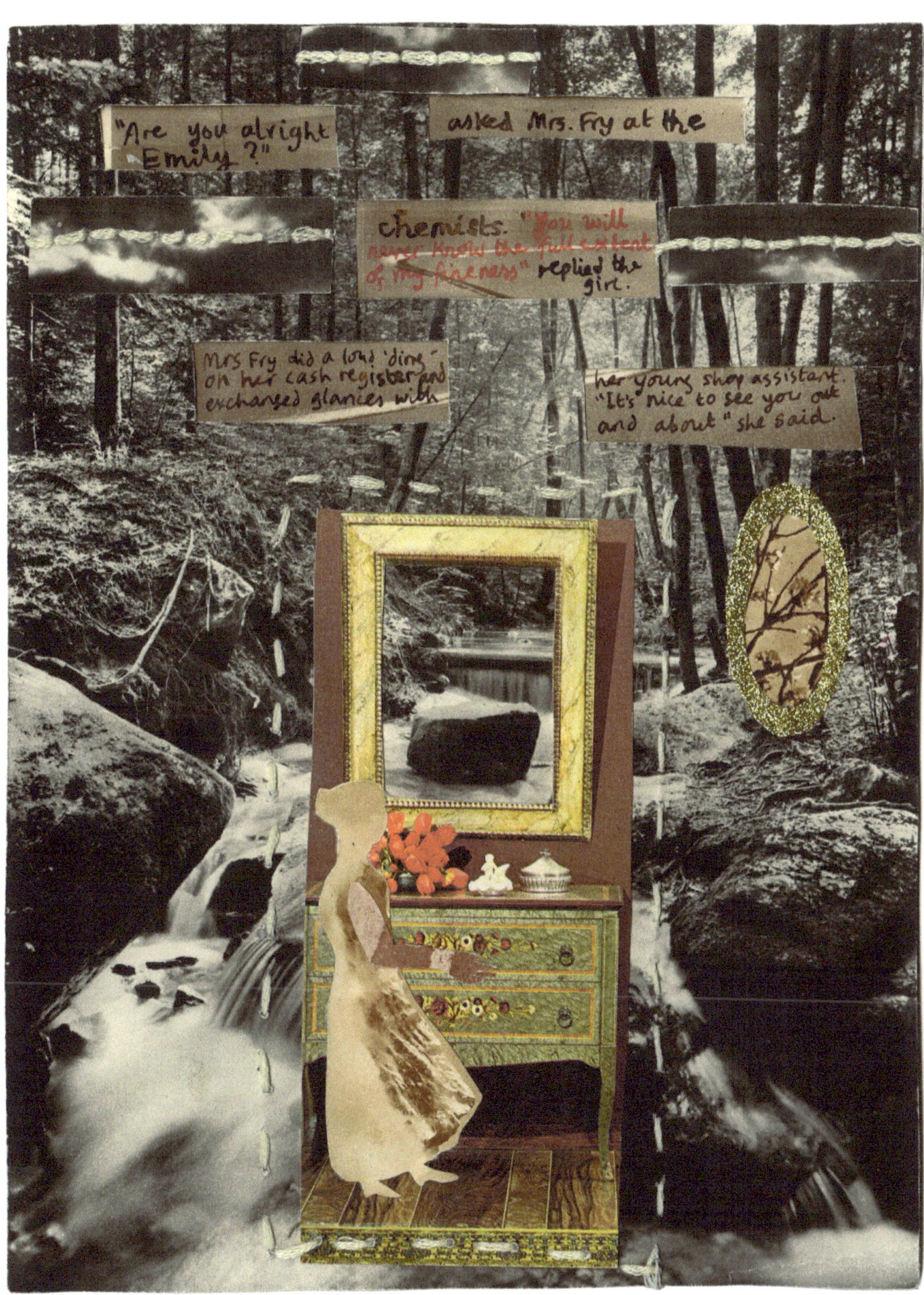

"Are you alright Emily?"
asked Mrs. Fry at the
chemists. "You will never know the full extent of my fineness" replied the girl.
Mrs Fry did a loud 'ding' on her cash register and exchanged glances with
her young shop assistant. "It's nice to see you out and about" she said.

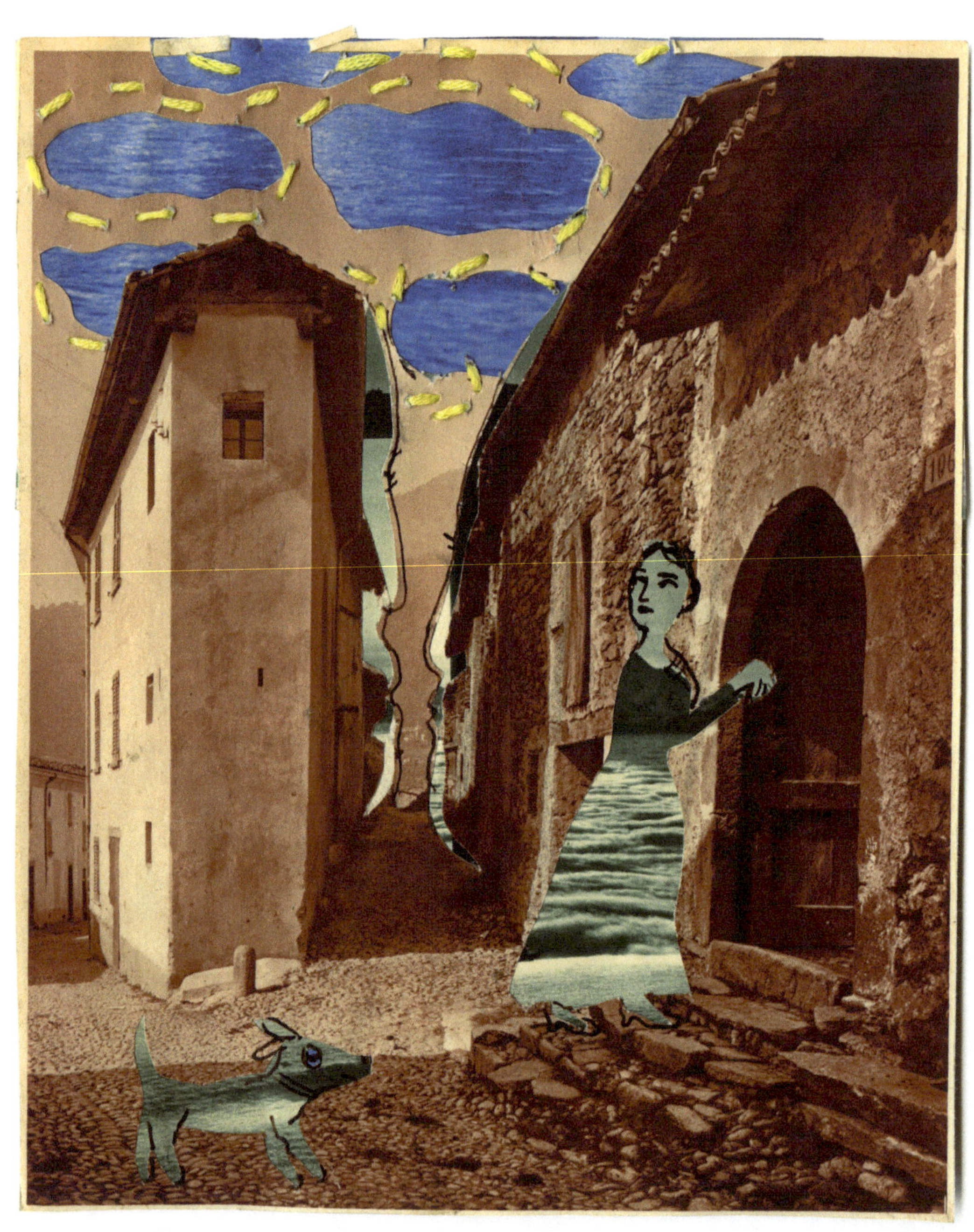

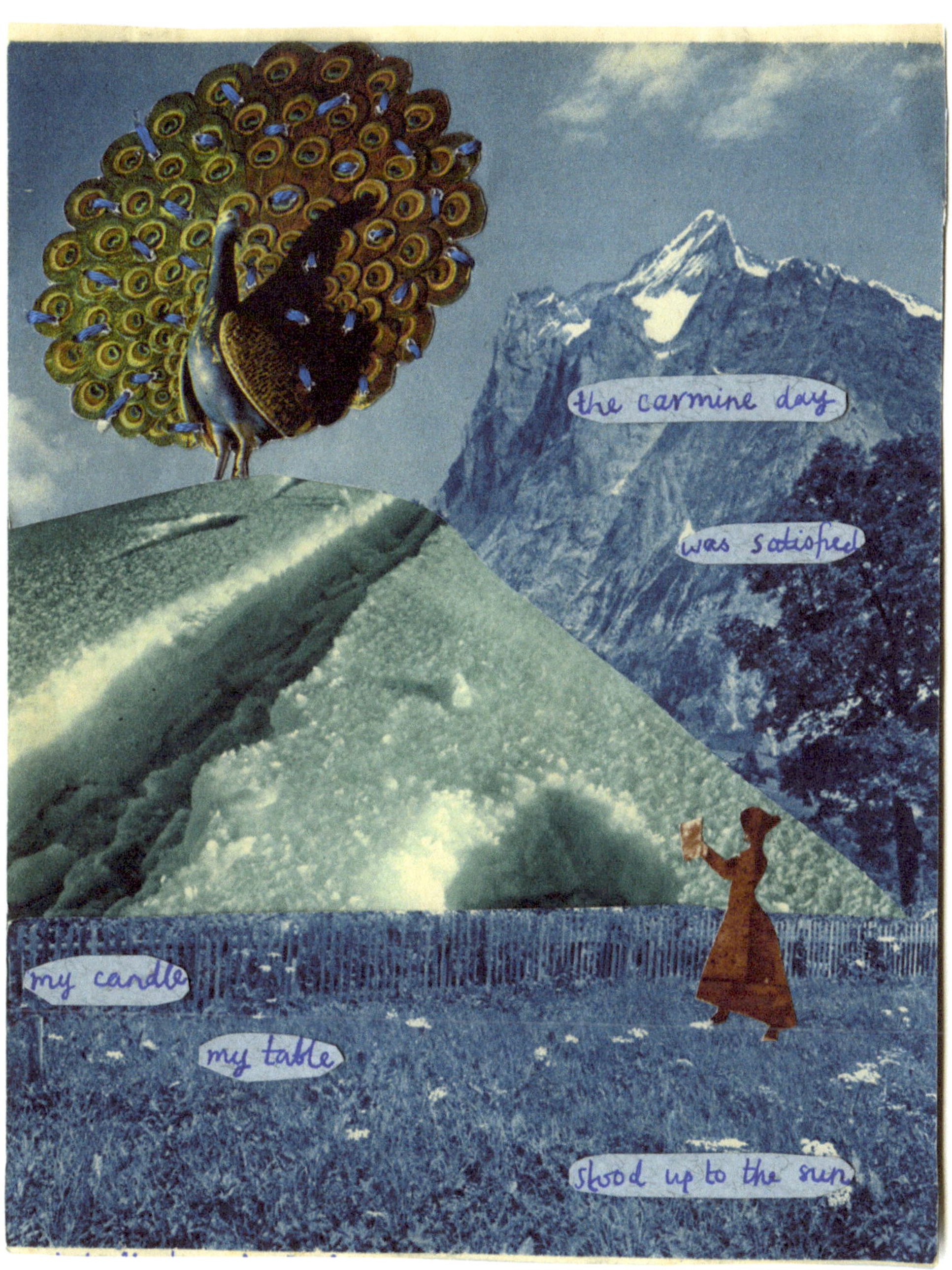
the carmine day
was satisfied
my candle
my table
stood up to the sun

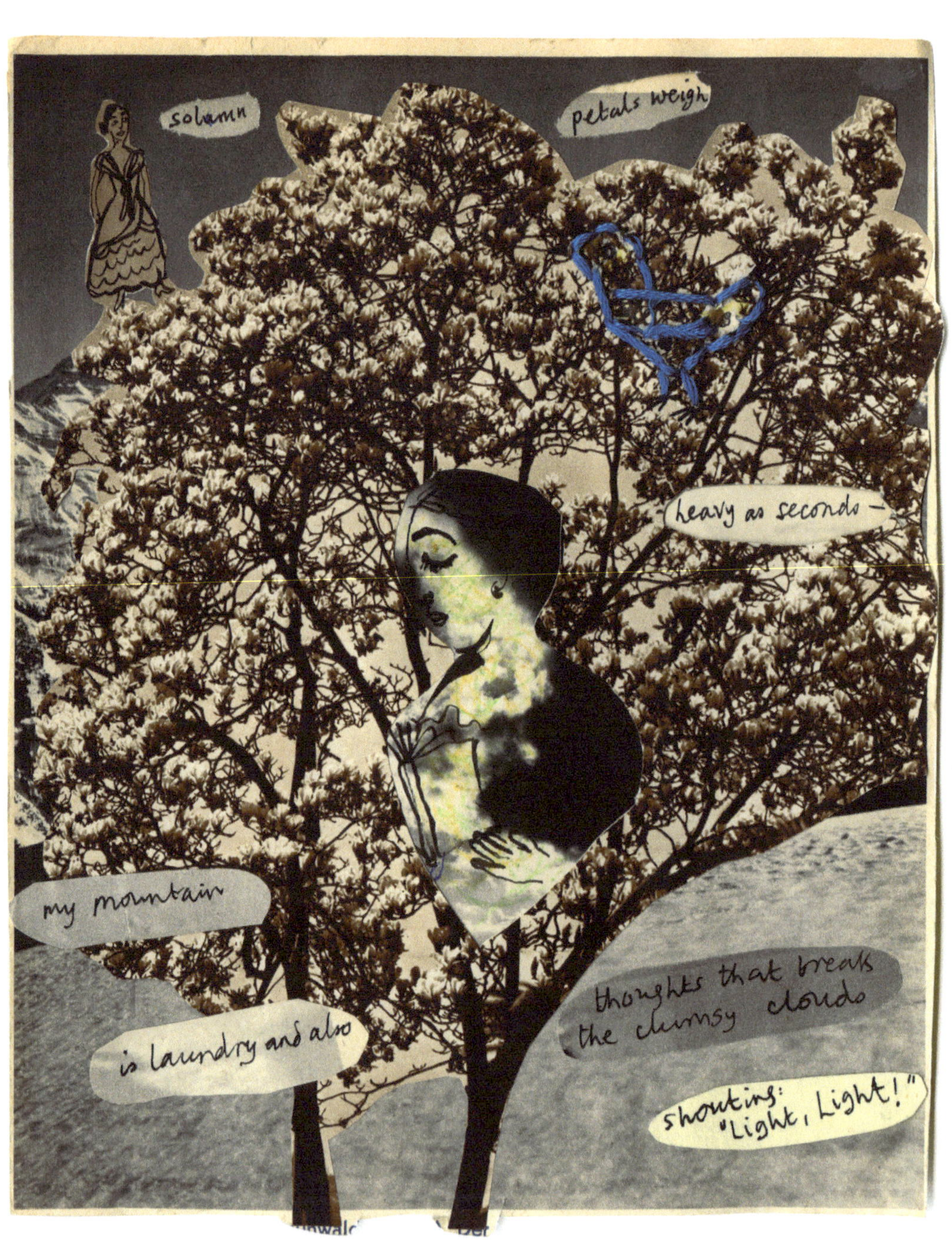

solumn
petals weigh
heavy as seconds —
my mountain
is laundry and also
thoughts that break
the clumsy clouds
shouting:
"Light, Light!"

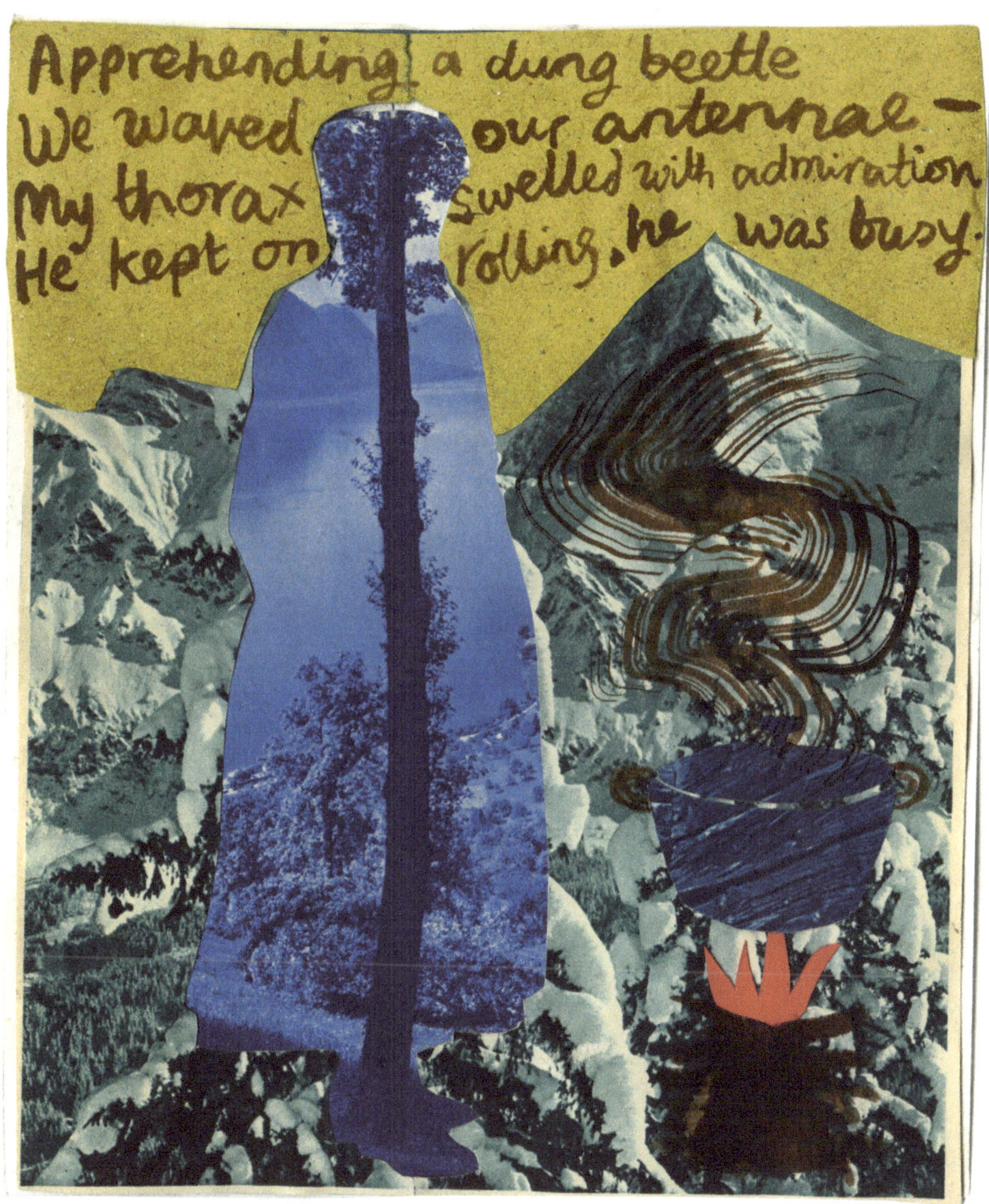

Apprehending a dung beetle
We waved our antennae —
My thorax swelled with admiration
He kept on rolling, he was busy.

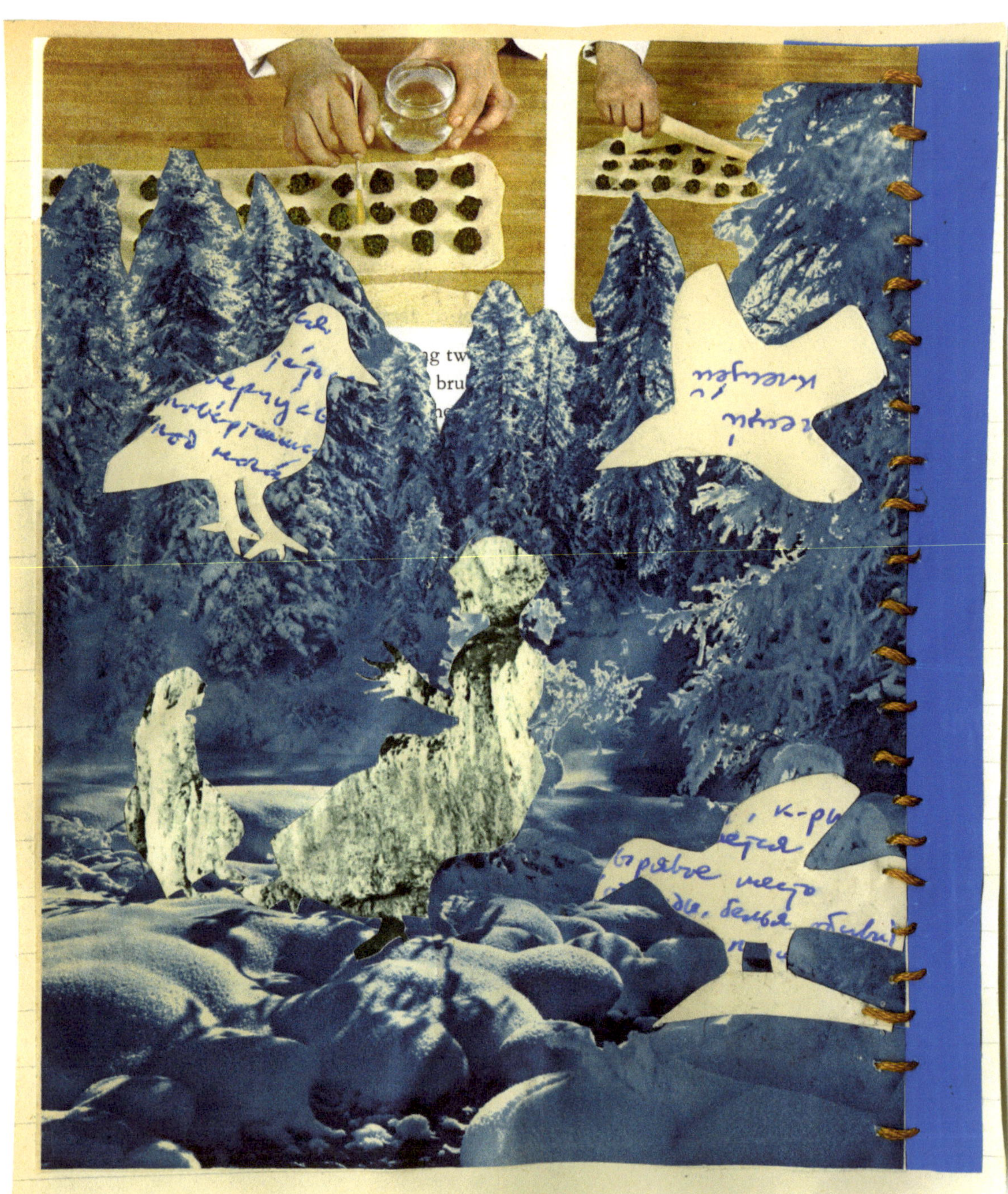

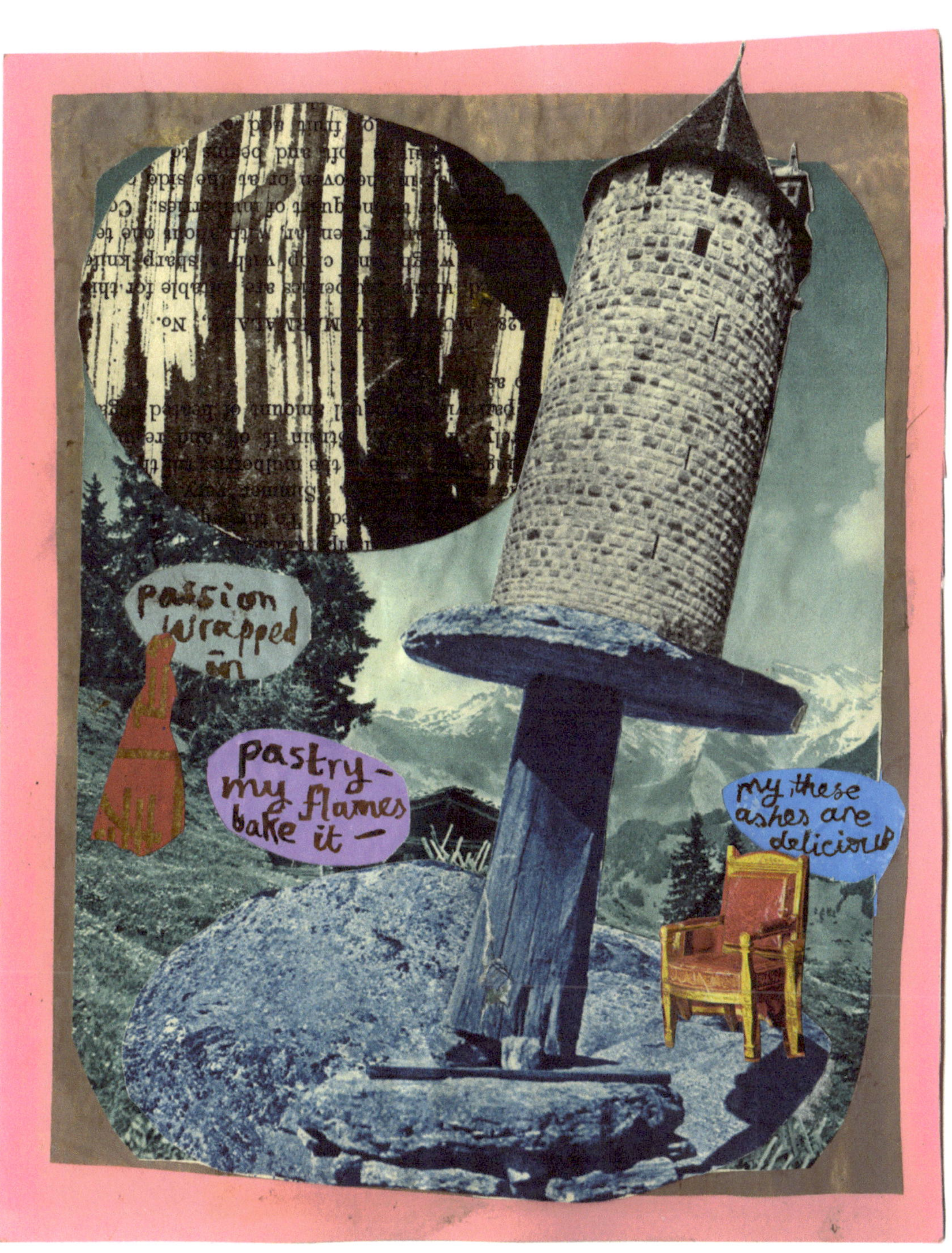

passion wrapped in
pastry — my flames bake it —
my these ashes are delicious

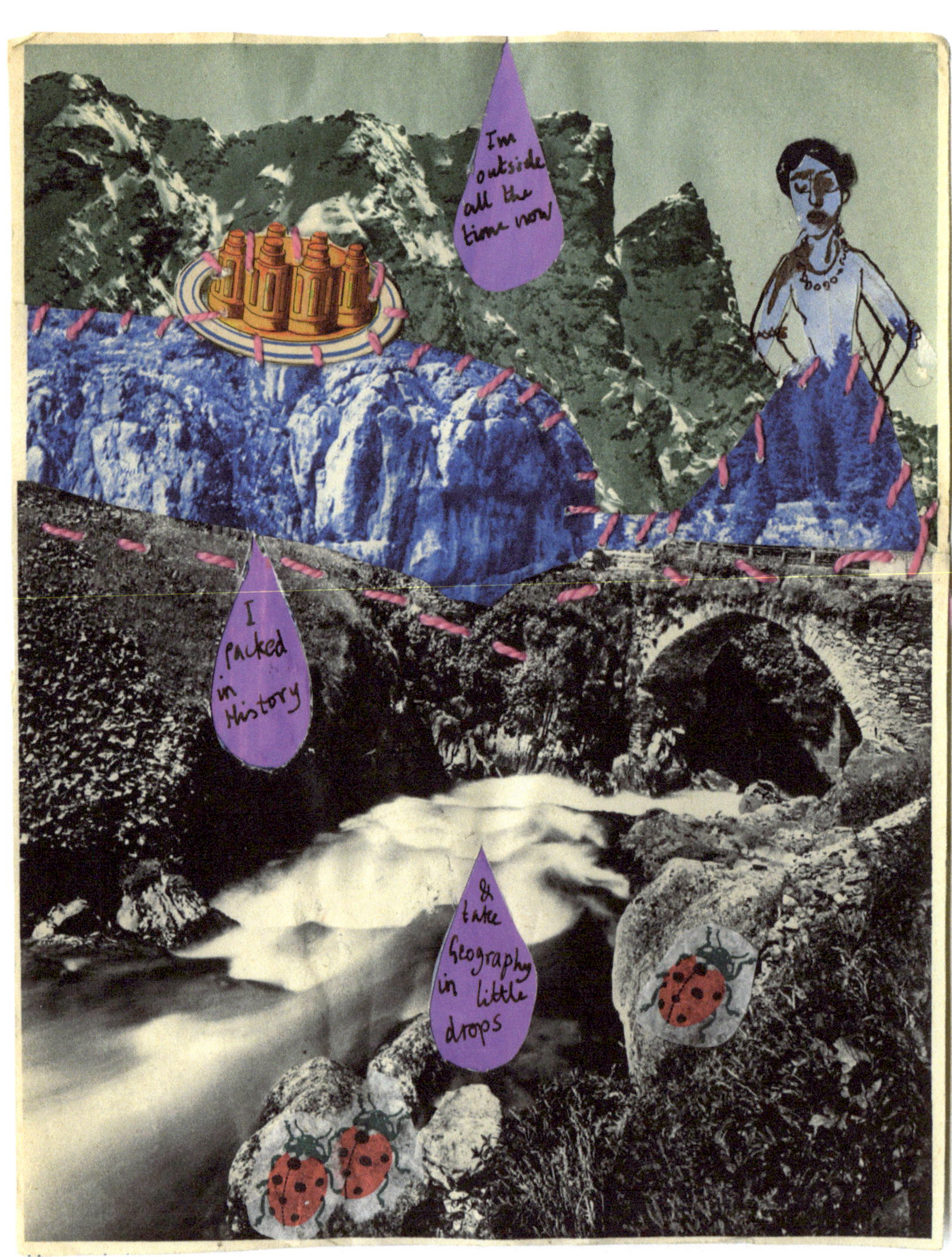

I'm outside all the time now
I packed in History
& take Geography in little drops

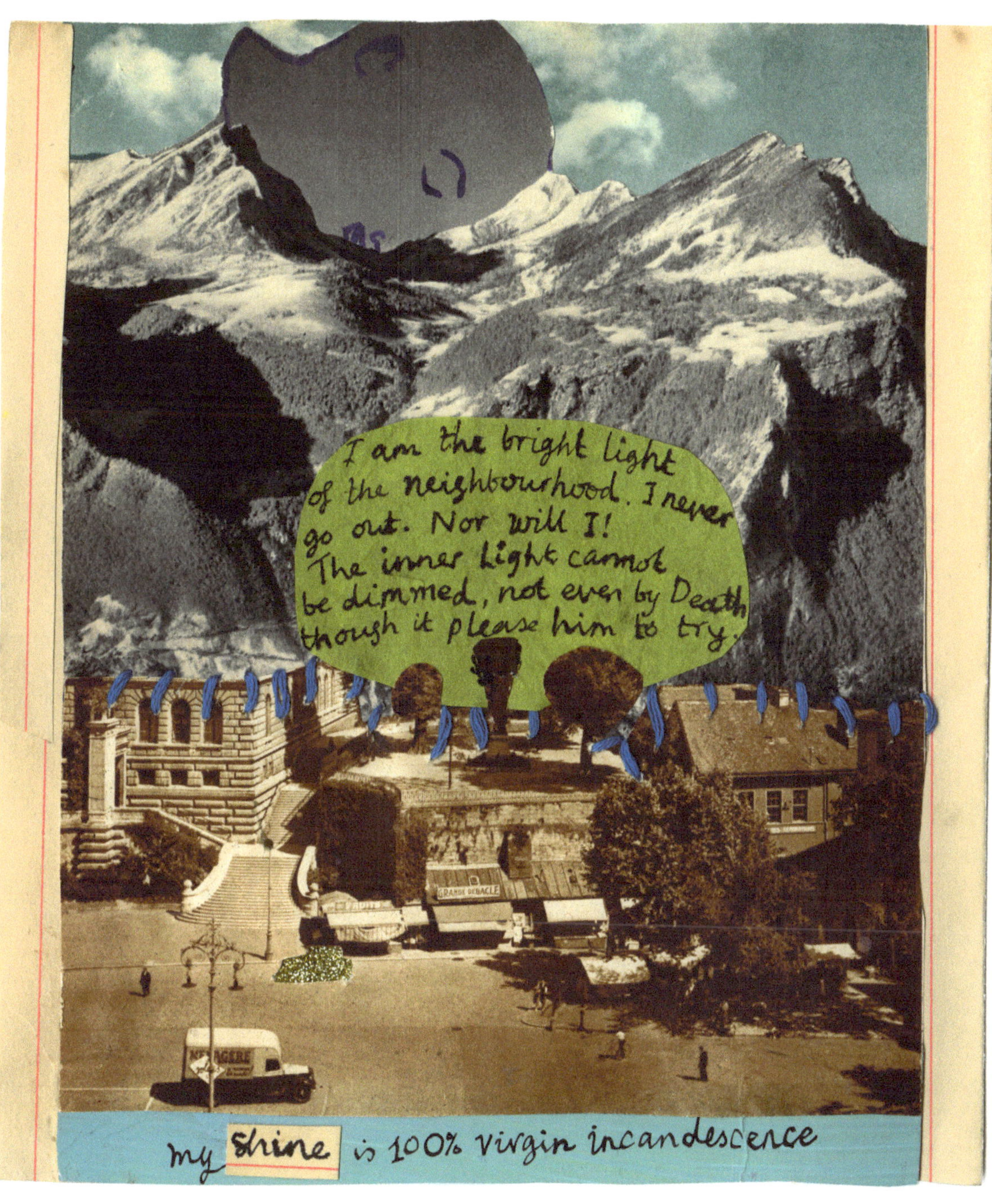

I am the bright light
of the neighbourhood. I never
go out. Nor will I!
The inner light cannot
be dimmed, not even by Death
though it please him to try.
my shine is 100% virgin incandescence

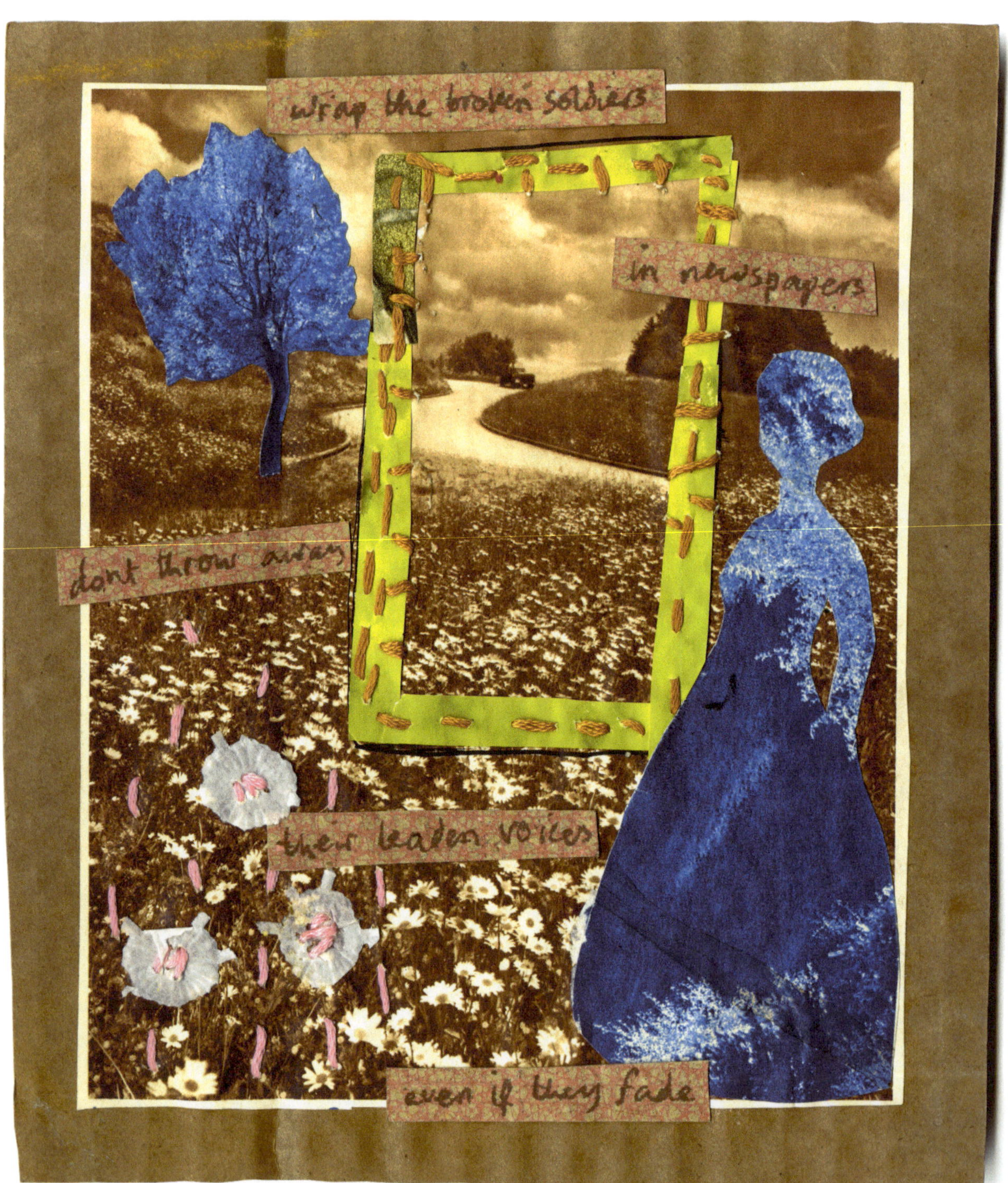

wrap the broken soldiers
in newspapers
dont throw away
their leaden voices
even if they fade

I made these collages in Spring 2017, set off by an Emily Dickinson
Instagram Poetry Competition call out from The Poetry School and
Soda Pictures UK. My own poems form part of the fabric of each work.

TO MY FRIEND Andy Davenport
    former flatmate and acknowledged genius, with love.

THANKS TO
Julia Bird, Sally Carruthers, John Canfield at the Poetry School.
Terence Davies, whose film about Emily: A Quiet Passion is brilliant.
Jean Gaberell, whose wonderful 1930s book of photographs I used
    as raw material.
Emily Dickinson herself, of course.
All who encouraged me by pressing 'like' on Instagram.
Thanks to The Art Stable in Dorset and to Aldeburgh Poetry Festival
    for exhibiting the originals.
Thanks to Can Binatli, Josh Baum, Sally Pomme Clayton, Abu Conteh,
Andy Davenport, David Henningham, Rosa Herxheimer, Chris McCabe,
Kelly Ross, Gigi Sudbury, Meryl Wilford, Alison Winch, and Adam
Unwin for helpful feedback and practical support.

Sophie Herxheimer, Brixton, June 2017

Published by Henningham Family Press, 2022
    henninghamfamilypress.co.uk

First published by Henningham Family Press 2017.
This edition is a machine produced version of the original handmade artists' book.

ISBN 9781916218659

British Library Cataloguing-in-publication Data
A catalogue record for this book is available from the British Library